"After utilizing toolkit resource, I was able to identify threats within my organization to which I was completely unaware. Using my team's knowledge as a competitive advantage, we now have superior systems that save time and energy."

"As a new Chief Technology Officer, I was feeling unprepared and inadequate to be successful in my role. I ordered an IT toolkit Sunday night and was prepared Monday morning to shed light on areas of improvement within my organization. I no longer felt overwhelmed and intimidated, I was excited to share what I had learned."

"I used the questionnaires to interview members of my team. I never knew how many insights we could produce collectively with our internal knowledge."

"I usually work until at least 8pm on weeknights. The Art of Service questionnaire saved me so much time and worry that Thursday night I attended my son's soccer game without sacrificing my professional obligations."

"After purchasing The Art of Service toolkit, I was able to identify areas where my company was not in compliance that could have put my job at risk. I looked like a hero when I proactively educated my team on the risks and presented a solid solution."

"I spent months shopping for an external consultant before realizing that The Art of Service would allow my team to consult themselves! Not only did we save time not catching a consultant up to speed, we were able to keep our company information and industry secrets confidential."

"Everyday there are new regulations and processes in my industry. The Art of Service toolkit has kept me ahead by using AI technology to constantly update the toolkits and address emerging needs."

"I customized The Art of Service toolkit to focus specifically on the concerns of my role and industry. I didn't have to waste time with a generic self-help book that wasn't tailored to my exact situation."

"Many of our competitors have asked us about our secret sauce. When I tell them it's the knowledge we have in-house, they never believe me. Little do they know The Art of Service toolkits are working behind the scenes."

"One of my friends hired a consultant who used the knowledge gained working with his company to advise their competitor. Talk about a competitive disadvantage! The Art of Service allowed us to keep our knowledge from walking out the door along with a huge portion of our budget in consulting fees."

"Honestly, I didn't know what I didn't know. Before purchasing The Art of Service, I didn't realize how many areas of my business needed to be refreshed and improved. I am so relieved The Art of Service was there to highlight our blind spots."

"Before The Art of Service, I waited eagerly for consulting company reports to come out each month. These reports kept us up to speed but provided little value because they put our competitors on the same playing field. With The Art of Service, we have uncovered unique insights to drive our business forward."

"Instead of investing extensive resources into an external consultant, we can spend more of our budget towards pursuing our company goals and objectives…while also spending a little more on corporate holiday parties."

"The risk of our competitors getting ahead has been mitigated because The Art of Service has provided us with a 360-degree view of threats within our organization before they even arise."

Incident and Crisis Management
Complete Self-Assessment Guide

Notice of rights

You are licensed to use the Self-Assessment contents in your presentations and materials for internal use and customers without asking us - we are here to help.

All rights reserved for the book itself: this book may not be reproduced or transmitted in any form by any means, electronic, mechanical, photocopying, recording, or otherwise, without the prior written permission of the publisher.

The information in this book is distributed on an "As Is" basis without warranty. While every precaution has been taken in the preparation of the book, neither the author nor the publisher shall have any liability to any person or entity with respect to any loss or damage caused or alleged to be caused directly or indirectly by the instructions contained in this book or by the products described in it.

Trademarks

Many of the designations used by manufacturers and sellers to distinguish their products are claimed as trademarks. Where those designations appear in this book, and the publisher was aware of a trademark claim, the designations appear as requested by the owner of the trademark. All other product names and services identified throughout this book are used in editorial fashion only and for the benefit of such companies with no intention of infringement of the trademark. No such use, or the use of any trade name, is intended to convey endorsement or other affiliation with this book.

Copyright © by The Art of Service
https://theartofservice.com
support@theartofservice.com

Table of Contents

About The Art of Service — 10

Included Resources - how to access — 10
Purpose of this Self-Assessment — 12
How to use the Self-Assessment — 13
Incident and Crisis Management Scorecard Example — 15
Incident and Crisis Management Scorecard — 16

BEGINNING OF THE SELF-ASSESSMENT: — 17
CRITERION #1: RECOGNIZE — 18

CRITERION #2: DEFINE: — 29

CRITERION #3: MEASURE: — 45

CRITERION #4: ANALYZE: — 60

CRITERION #5: IMPROVE: — 76

CRITERION #6: CONTROL: — 92

CRITERION #7: SUSTAIN: — 105
Incident and Crisis Management and Managing Projects, Criteria for Project Managers: — 133
1.0 Initiating Process Group: Incident and Crisis Management — 134

1.1 Project Charter: Incident and Crisis Management — 136

1.2 Stakeholder Register: Incident and Crisis Management — 138

1.3 Stakeholder Analysis Matrix: Incident and Crisis Management — 139

2.0 Planning Process Group: Incident and Crisis Management 141

2.1 Project Management Plan: Incident and Crisis Management 144

2.2 Scope Management Plan: Incident and Crisis Management 146

2.3 Requirements Management Plan: Incident and Crisis Management 148

2.4 Requirements Documentation: Incident and Crisis Management 150

2.5 Requirements Traceability Matrix: Incident and Crisis Management 152

2.6 Project Scope Statement: Incident and Crisis Management 154

2.7 Assumption and Constraint Log: Incident and Crisis Management 157

2.8 Work Breakdown Structure: Incident and Crisis Management 159

2.9 WBS Dictionary: Incident and Crisis Management 161

2.10 Schedule Management Plan: Incident and Crisis Management 164

2.11 Activity List: Incident and Crisis Management 166

2.12 Activity Attributes: Incident and Crisis Management 168

2.13 Milestone List: Incident and Crisis Management 170

2.14 Network Diagram: Incident and Crisis Management 172

2.15 Activity Resource Requirements: Incident and Crisis Management 174

2.16 Resource Breakdown Structure: Incident and Crisis Management 175

2.17 Activity Duration Estimates: Incident and Crisis Management 177

2.18 Duration Estimating Worksheet: Incident and Crisis Management 180

2.19 Project Schedule: Incident and Crisis Management 182

2.20 Cost Management Plan: Incident and Crisis Management 184

2.21 Activity Cost Estimates: Incident and Crisis Management 186

2.22 Cost Estimating Worksheet: Incident and Crisis Management 188

2.23 Cost Baseline: Incident and Crisis Management 190

2.24 Quality Management Plan: Incident and Crisis Management 192

2.25 Quality Metrics: Incident and Crisis Management 194

2.26 Process Improvement Plan: Incident and Crisis Management 196

2.27 Responsibility Assignment Matrix: Incident and Crisis Management 198

2.28 Roles and Responsibilities: Incident and Crisis Management — 200

2.29 Human Resource Management Plan: Incident and Crisis Management — 202

2.30 Communications Management Plan: Incident and Crisis Management — 204

2.31 Risk Management Plan: Incident and Crisis Management — 206

2.32 Risk Register: Incident and Crisis Management — 208

2.33 Probability and Impact Assessment: Incident and Crisis Management — 210

2.34 Probability and Impact Matrix: Incident and Crisis Management — 212

2.35 Risk Data Sheet: Incident and Crisis Management — 214

2.36 Procurement Management Plan: Incident and Crisis Management — 216

2.37 Source Selection Criteria: Incident and Crisis Management — 218

2.38 Stakeholder Management Plan: Incident and Crisis Management — 220

2.39 Change Management Plan: Incident and Crisis Management — 222

3.0 Executing Process Group: Incident and Crisis Management — 224

3.1 Team Member Status Report: Incident and Crisis Management 226

3.2 Change Request: Incident and Crisis Management 228

3.3 Change Log: Incident and Crisis Management 230

3.4 Decision Log: Incident and Crisis Management 232

3.5 Quality Audit: Incident and Crisis Management 234

3.6 Team Directory: Incident and Crisis Management 236

3.7 Team Operating Agreement: Incident and Crisis Management 238

3.8 Team Performance Assessment: Incident and Crisis Management 240

3.9 Team Member Performance Assessment: Incident and Crisis Management 242

3.10 Issue Log: Incident and Crisis Management 244

4.0 Monitoring and Controlling Process Group: Incident and Crisis Management 246

4.1 Project Performance Report: Incident and Crisis Management 248

4.2 Variance Analysis: Incident and Crisis Management 250

4.3 Earned Value Status: Incident and Crisis Management 252

4.4 Risk Audit: Incident and Crisis Management 254

4.5 Contractor Status Report: Incident and Crisis Management 256

4.6 Formal Acceptance: Incident and Crisis Management 258

5.0 Closing Process Group: Incident and Crisis Management 260

5.1 Procurement Audit: Incident and Crisis Management 262

5.2 Contract Close-Out: Incident and Crisis Management 265

5.3 Project or Phase Close-Out: Incident and Crisis Management 267

5.4 Lessons Learned: Incident and Crisis Management 269
Index 271

About The Art of Service

The Art of Service, Business Process Architects since 2000, is dedicated to helping stakeholders achieve excellence.

Defining, designing, creating, and implementing a process to solve a stakeholders challenge or meet an objective is the most valuable role… In EVERY group, company, organization and department.

Unless you're talking a one-time, single-use project, there should be a process. Whether that process is managed and implemented by humans, AI, or a combination of the two, it needs to be designed by someone with a complex enough perspective to ask the right questions.

Someone capable of asking the right questions and step back and say, 'What are we really trying to accomplish here? And is there a different way to look at it?'

With The Art of Service's Self-Assessments, we empower people who can do just that — whether their title is marketer, entrepreneur, manager, salesperson, consultant, Business Process Manager, executive assistant, IT Manager, CIO etc... —they are the people who rule the future. They are people who watch the process as it happens, and ask the right questions to make the process work better.

Contact us when you need any support with this Self-Assessment and any help with templates, blue-prints and examples of standard documents you might need:

https://theartofservice.com
support@theartofservice.com

Included Resources - how to access

Included with your purchase of the book is the Incident and

Crisis Management Self-Assessment Spreadsheet Dashboard which contains all questions and Self-Assessment areas and auto-generates insights, graphs, and project RACI planning - all with examples to get you started right away.

How? Simply send an email to
access@theartofservice.com
with this books' title in the subject to get the Incident and Crisis Management Self Assessment Tool right away.

The auto reply will guide you further, you will then receive the following contents with New and Updated specific criteria:

- The latest quick edition of the book in PDF

- The latest complete edition of the book in PDF, which criteria correspond to the criteria in…

- The Self-Assessment Excel Dashboard, and…

- Example pre-filled Self-Assessment Excel Dashboard to get familiar with results generation

- In-depth specific Checklists covering the topic

- Project management checklists and templates to assist with implementation

INCLUDES LIFETIME SELF ASSESSMENT UPDATES

Every self assessment comes with Lifetime Updates and Lifetime Free Updated Books. Lifetime Updates is an industry-first feature which allows you to receive verified self assessment updates, ensuring you always have the most accurate information at your fingertips.

Get it now- you will be glad you did - do it now, before you forget.

Send an email to **access@theartofservice.com** with this books' title in the subject to get the Incident and Crisis Management Self Assessment Tool right away.

Purpose of this Self-Assessment

This Self-Assessment has been developed to improve understanding of the requirements and elements of Incident and Crisis Management, based on best practices and standards in business process architecture, design and quality management.

It is designed to allow for a rapid Self-Assessment to determine how closely existing management practices and procedures correspond to the elements of the Self-Assessment.

The criteria of requirements and elements of Incident and Crisis Management have been rephrased in the format of a Self-Assessment questionnaire, with a seven-criterion scoring system, as explained in this document.

In this format, even with limited background knowledge of Incident and Crisis Management, a manager can quickly review existing operations to determine how they measure up to the standards. This in turn can serve as the starting point of a 'gap analysis' to identify management tools or system elements that might usefully be implemented in the organization to help improve overall performance.

How to use the Self-Assessment

On the following pages are a series of questions to identify to what extent your Incident and Crisis Management initiative is complete in comparison to the requirements set in standards.

To facilitate answering the questions, there is a space in front of each question to enter a score on a scale of '1' to '5'.

> 1 Strongly Disagree
>
> 2 Disagree
>
> 3 Neutral
>
> 4 Agree
>
> 5 Strongly Agree

Read the question and rate it with the following in front of mind:

'In my belief, the answer to this question is clearly defined'.

There are two ways in which you can choose to interpret this statement;
1. how aware are you that the answer to the question is clearly defined
2. for more in-depth analysis you can choose to gather evidence and confirm the answer to the question. This obviously will take more time, most Self-Assessment users opt for the first way to interpret the question and dig deeper later on based on the outcome of the overall Self-Assessment.

A score of '1' would mean that the answer is not clear at all, where a '5' would mean the answer is crystal clear and defined. Leave emtpy when the question is not applicable or you don't want to answer it, you can skip it without affecting your score. Write your score in the space provided.

After you have responded to all the appropriate statements in each section, compute your average score for that section, using the formula provided, and round to the nearest tenth. Then transfer to the corresponding spoke in the Incident and Crisis Management Scorecard on the second next page of the Self-Assessment.

Your completed Incident and Crisis Management Scorecard will give you a clear presentation of which Incident and Crisis Management areas need attention.

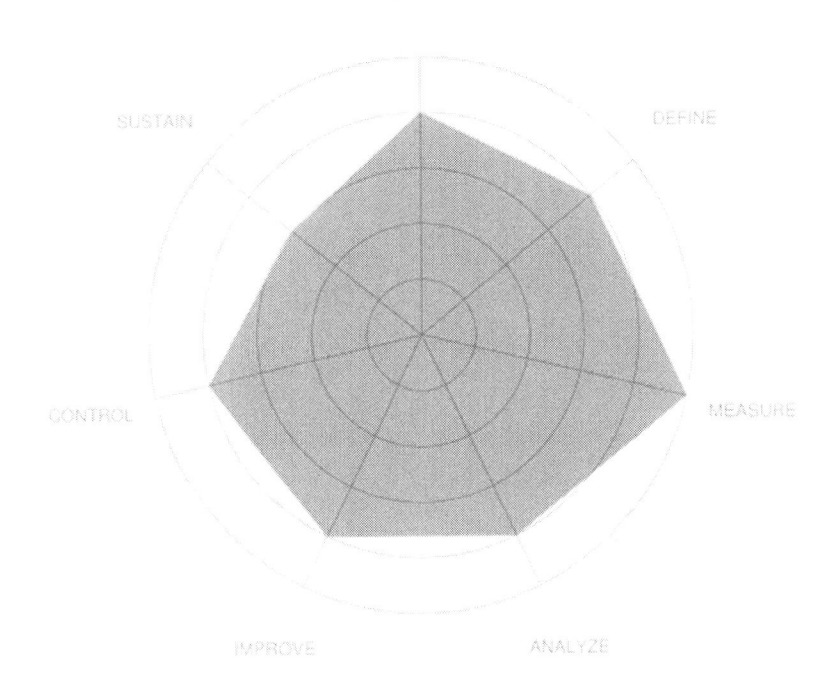

Incident and Crisis Management Scorecard Example

Example of how the finalized Scorecard can look like:

Incident and Crisis Management Scorecard

Your Scores:

RECOGNIZE

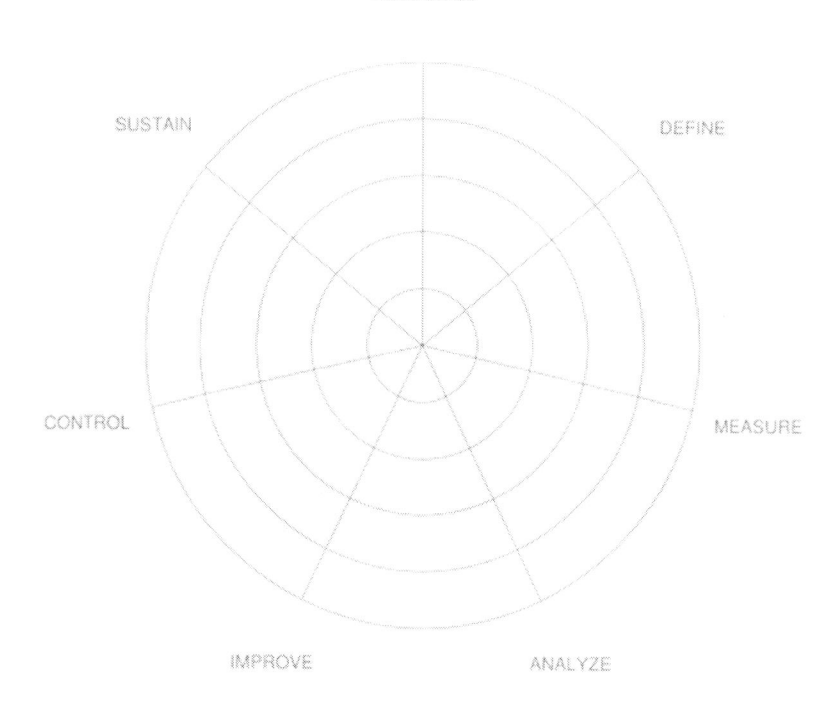

SUSTAIN

DEFINE

CONTROL

MEASURE

IMPROVE

ANALYZE

BEGINNING OF THE SELF-ASSESSMENT:

CRITERION #1: RECOGNIZE

INTENT: Be aware of the need for change. Recognize that there is an unfavorable variation, problem or symptom.

In my belief, the answer to this question is clearly defined:

5 Strongly Agree

4 Agree

3 Neutral

2 Disagree

1 Strongly Disagree

1. What Incident and Crisis Management events should you attend?
<--- Score

2. To what extent does each concerned units management team recognize Incident and Crisis Management as an effective investment?
<--- Score

3. Are controls defined to recognize and contain problems?
<--- Score

4. Do you know what you need to know about Incident and Crisis Management?
<--- Score

5. Are there any revenue recognition issues?
<--- Score

6. How does it fit into your organizational needs and tasks?
<--- Score

7. What is the Incident and Crisis Management problem definition? What do you need to resolve?
<--- Score

8. What is the smallest subset of the problem you can usefully solve?
<--- Score

9. What are the Incident and Crisis Management resources needed?
<--- Score

10. How are you going to measure success?
<--- Score

11. Will a response program recognize when a crisis occurs and provide some level of response?
<--- Score

12. What are the minority interests and what amount of minority interests can be recognized?

<--- Score

13. What are the clients issues and concerns?
<--- Score

14. How much are sponsors, customers, partners, stakeholders involved in Incident and Crisis Management? In other words, what are the risks, if Incident and Crisis Management does not deliver successfully?
<--- Score

15. Are employees recognized or rewarded for performance that demonstrates the highest levels of integrity?
<--- Score

16. Will Incident and Crisis Management deliverables need to be tested and, if so, by whom?
<--- Score

17. What are the stakeholder objectives to be achieved with Incident and Crisis Management?
<--- Score

18. What training and capacity building actions are needed to implement proposed reforms?
<--- Score

19. What Incident and Crisis Management coordination do you need?
<--- Score

20. What should be considered when identifying available resources, constraints, and deadlines?
<--- Score

21. Consider your own Incident and Crisis Management project, what types of organizational problems do you think might be causing or affecting your problem, based on the work done so far?
<--- Score

22. What are the expected benefits of Incident and Crisis Management to the stakeholder?
<--- Score

23. How do you recognize an Incident and Crisis Management objection?
<--- Score

24. Can management personnel recognize the monetary benefit of Incident and Crisis Management?
<--- Score

25. Does Incident and Crisis Management create potential expectations in other areas that need to be recognized and considered?
<--- Score

26. Who else hopes to benefit from it?
<--- Score

27. How are the Incident and Crisis Management's objectives aligned to the group's overall stakeholder strategy?
<--- Score

28. Did you miss any major Incident and Crisis Management issues?
<--- Score

29. What are the timeframes required to resolve each of the issues/problems?
<--- Score

30. What extra resources will you need?
<--- Score

31. What is the extent or complexity of the Incident and Crisis Management problem?
<--- Score

32. What Incident and Crisis Management capabilities do you need?
<--- Score

33. Is it needed?
<--- Score

34. Are there any specific expectations or concerns about the Incident and Crisis Management team, Incident and Crisis Management itself?
<--- Score

35. Which issues are too important to ignore?
<--- Score

36. Are your goals realistic? Do you need to redefine your problem? Perhaps the problem has changed or maybe you have reached your goal and need to set a new one?
<--- Score

37. Do you need to avoid or amend any Incident and Crisis Management activities?
<--- Score

38. As a sponsor, customer or management, how important is it to meet goals, objectives?
<--- Score

39. Is it clear when you think of the day ahead of you what activities and tasks you need to complete?
<--- Score

40. Who defines the rules in relation to any given issue?
<--- Score

41. Do you need different information or graphics?
<--- Score

42. How do you recognize an objection?
<--- Score

43. What is a realistic assessment of related safety issues?
<--- Score

44. Looking at each person individually – does every one have the qualities which are needed to work in this group?
<--- Score

45. How do you take a forward-looking perspective in identifying Incident and Crisis Management research related to market response and models?
<--- Score

46. What tools and technologies are needed for a custom Incident and Crisis Management project?
<--- Score

47. What is the problem or issue?
<--- Score

48. For your Incident and Crisis Management project, identify and describe the business environment, is there more than one layer to the business environment?
<--- Score

49. Are you dealing with any of the same issues today as yesterday? What can you do about this?
<--- Score

50. Whom do you really need or want to serve?
<--- Score

51. How are training requirements identified?
<--- Score

52. Think about the people you identified for your Incident and Crisis Management project and the project responsibilities you would assign to them, what kind of training do you think they would need to perform these responsibilities effectively?
<--- Score

53. Would you recognize a threat from the inside?
<--- Score

54. What else needs to be measured?
<--- Score

55. What problems are you facing and how do you consider Incident and Crisis Management will circumvent those obstacles?
<--- Score

56. Does your organization need more Incident and Crisis Management education?
<--- Score

57. What kinds of emergency services are needed during and after an emergency?
<--- Score

58. Who else might you need to collaborate with regarding communications?
<--- Score

59. Will new equipment/products be required to facilitate Incident and Crisis Management delivery, for example is new software needed?
<--- Score

60. Do you have/need 24-hour access to key personnel?
<--- Score

61. How many trainings, in total, are needed?
<--- Score

62. Where do you need to exercise leadership?
<--- Score

63. To what extent would your organization benefit from being recognized as a award recipient?
<--- Score

64. Are problem definition and motivation clearly presented?
<--- Score

65. Are there any positive stories to issue?
<--- Score

66. What creative shifts do you need to take?
<--- Score

67. What do you need to start doing?
<--- Score

68. What is the recognized need?
<--- Score

69. Are there Incident and Crisis Management problems defined?
<--- Score

70. Which information does the Incident and Crisis Management business case need to include?
<--- Score

71. How do you identify subcontractor relationships?
<--- Score

72. Who needs what information?
<--- Score

73. Who needs budgets?
<--- Score

74. What is the problem and/or vulnerability?
<--- Score

75. Will it solve real problems?
<--- Score

76. What are your needs in relation to Incident and

Crisis Management skills, labor, equipment, and markets?
<--- Score

77. What would happen if Incident and Crisis Management weren't done?
<--- Score

78. When a Incident and Crisis Management manager recognizes a problem, what options are available?
<--- Score

79. Do you recognize Incident and Crisis Management achievements?
<--- Score

80. Why the need?
<--- Score

81. What situation(s) led to this Incident and Crisis Management Self Assessment?
<--- Score

82. What does Incident and Crisis Management success mean to the stakeholders?
<--- Score

83. Who should resolve the Incident and Crisis Management issues?
<--- Score

84. How do you assess your Incident and Crisis Management workforce capability and capacity needs, including skills, competencies, and staffing levels?
<--- Score

85. Are there recognized Incident and Crisis Management problems?
<--- Score

86. Is the need for organizational change recognized?
<--- Score

87. What do employees need in the short term?
<--- Score

88. Are there regulatory / compliance issues?
<--- Score

89. Who are your key stakeholders who need to sign off?
<--- Score

90. Who needs to know?
<--- Score

Add up total points for this section:
_____ = Total points for this section

Divided by: _____ (number of statements answered) = _____
Average score for this section

Transfer your score to the Incident and Crisis Management Index at the beginning of the Self-Assessment.

CRITERION #2: DEFINE:

INTENT: Formulate the stakeholder problem. Define the problem, needs and objectives.

In my belief, the answer to this question is clearly defined:

5 Strongly Agree

4 Agree

3 Neutral

2 Disagree

1 Strongly Disagree

1. How can the value of Incident and Crisis Management be defined?
<--- Score

2. What knowledge or experience is required?
<--- Score

3. Is there a Incident and Crisis Management management charter, including stakeholder case,

problem and goal statements, scope, milestones, roles and responsibilities, communication plan?
<--- Score

4. Who is gathering information?
<--- Score

5. Are different versions of process maps needed to account for the different types of inputs?
<--- Score

6. Do you have a Incident and Crisis Management success story or case study ready to tell and share?
<--- Score

7. Is data collected and displayed to better understand customer(s) critical needs and requirements.
<--- Score

8. What key stakeholder process output measure(s) does Incident and Crisis Management leverage and how?
<--- Score

9. Who approved the Incident and Crisis Management scope?
<--- Score

10. Is the work to date meeting requirements?
<--- Score

11. Do you or your visitors require any urgent assistance?
<--- Score

12. How do you gather Incident and Crisis

Management requirements?
<--- Score

13. Will team members perform Incident and Crisis Management work when assigned and in a timely fashion?
<--- Score

14. What is the definition of Incident and Crisis Management excellence?
<--- Score

15. What system do you use for gathering Incident and Crisis Management information?
<--- Score

16. Is scope creep really all bad news?
<--- Score

17. How will variation in the actual durations of each activity be dealt with to ensure that the expected Incident and Crisis Management results are met?
<--- Score

18. Do the problem and goal statements meet the SMART criteria (specific, measurable, attainable, relevant, and time-bound)?
<--- Score

19. Is Incident and Crisis Management linked to key stakeholder goals and objectives?
<--- Score

20. What Incident and Crisis Management services do you require?
<--- Score

21. What happens if Incident and Crisis Management's scope changes?
<--- Score

22. What sources do you use to gather information for a Incident and Crisis Management study?
<--- Score

23. Are accountability and ownership for Incident and Crisis Management clearly defined?
<--- Score

24. Has the direction changed at all during the course of Incident and Crisis Management? If so, when did it change and why?
<--- Score

25. Is there a completed SIPOC representation, describing the Suppliers, Inputs, Process, Outputs, and Customers?
<--- Score

26. Have all of the relationships been defined properly?
<--- Score

27. What would be the goal or target for a Incident and Crisis Management's improvement team?
<--- Score

28. Who are the Incident and Crisis Management improvement team members, including Management Leads and Coaches?
<--- Score

29. What is a worst-case scenario for losses?
<--- Score

30. Has a project plan, Gantt chart, or similar been developed/completed?
<--- Score

31. What defines best in class?
<--- Score

32. Are there any constraints known that bear on the ability to perform Incident and Crisis Management work? How is the team addressing them?
<--- Score

33. What are the requirements for audit information?
<--- Score

34. What are the rough order estimates on cost savings/opportunities that Incident and Crisis Management brings?
<--- Score

35. How does the Incident and Crisis Management manager ensure against scope creep?
<--- Score

36. What are the compelling stakeholder reasons for embarking on Incident and Crisis Management?
<--- Score

37. How do you catch Incident and Crisis Management definition inconsistencies?
<--- Score

38. Have specific policy objectives been defined?

<--- Score

39. What is the scope?
<--- Score

40. Is the team equipped with available and reliable resources?
<--- Score

41. When are meeting minutes sent out? Who is on the distribution list?
<--- Score

42. Is full participation by members in regularly held team meetings guaranteed?
<--- Score

43. Do you all define Incident and Crisis Management in the same way?
<--- Score

44. Are audit criteria, scope, frequency and methods defined?
<--- Score

45. What information should you gather?
<--- Score

46. Are required metrics defined, what are they?
<--- Score

47. Have all basic functions of Incident and Crisis Management been defined?
<--- Score

48. Are customers identified and high impact areas

defined?
<--- Score

49. How do you manage scope?
<--- Score

50. What are the record-keeping requirements of Incident and Crisis Management activities?
<--- Score

51. What information do you gather?
<--- Score

52. What is in the scope and what is not in scope?
<--- Score

53. Where can you gather more information?
<--- Score

54. Has the improvement team collected the 'voice of the customer' (obtained feedback – qualitative and quantitative)?
<--- Score

55. What scope to assess?
<--- Score

56. How would you define the culture at your organization, how susceptible is it to Incident and Crisis Management changes?
<--- Score

57. Is the team formed and are team leaders (Coaches and Management Leads) assigned?
<--- Score

58. What are (control) requirements for Incident and Crisis Management Information?
<--- Score

59. What customer feedback methods were used to solicit their input?
<--- Score

60. What was the context?
<--- Score

61. What are the boundaries of the scope? What is in bounds and what is not? What is the start point? What is the stop point?
<--- Score

62. How do you think the partners involved in Incident and Crisis Management would have defined success?
<--- Score

63. How do you hand over Incident and Crisis Management context?
<--- Score

64. Does the scope remain the same?
<--- Score

65. Does the team have regular meetings?
<--- Score

66. How and when will the baselines be defined?
<--- Score

67. What intelligence can you gather?
<--- Score

68. Do you have organizational privacy requirements?
<--- Score

69. What critical content must be communicated – who, what, when, where, and how?
<--- Score

70. What is the scope of the Incident and Crisis Management effort?
<--- Score

71. Has the Incident and Crisis Management work been fairly and/or equitably divided and delegated among team members who are qualified and capable to perform the work? Has everyone contributed?
<--- Score

72. What scope do you want your strategy to cover?
<--- Score

73. Who defines (or who defined) the rules and roles?
<--- Score

74. What are the tasks and definitions?
<--- Score

75. Is the improvement team aware of the different versions of a process: what they think it is vs. what it actually is vs. what it should be vs. what it could be?
<--- Score

76. If substitutes have been appointed, have they been briefed on the Incident and Crisis Management goals and received regular communications as to the progress to date?

<--- Score

77. Will team members regularly document their Incident and Crisis Management work?
<--- Score

78. What is the definition of success?
<--- Score

79. Is Incident and Crisis Management currently on schedule according to the plan?
<--- Score

80. What are the Incident and Crisis Management tasks and definitions?
<--- Score

81. Are there different segments of customers?
<--- Score

82. How do you gather requirements?
<--- Score

83. When is/was the Incident and Crisis Management start date?
<--- Score

84. Is the Incident and Crisis Management scope manageable?
<--- Score

85. Is there a critical path to deliver Incident and Crisis Management results?
<--- Score

86. What is the worst-case scenario here?

<--- Score

87. What are the dynamics of the communication plan?
<--- Score

88. Have the customer needs been translated into specific, measurable requirements? How?
<--- Score

89. How do you gather the stories?
<--- Score

90. Is the team sponsored by a champion or stakeholder leader?
<--- Score

91. Who is gathering Incident and Crisis Management information?
<--- Score

92. How do you manage changes in Incident and Crisis Management requirements?
<--- Score

93. Are customer(s) identified and segmented according to their different needs and requirements?
<--- Score

94. Are the Incident and Crisis Management requirements testable?
<--- Score

95. How do you manage unclear Incident and Crisis Management requirements?
<--- Score

96. Is the current 'as is' process being followed? If not, what are the discrepancies?
<--- Score

97. In what way can you redefine the criteria of choice clients have in your category in your favor?
<--- Score

98. Are stakeholder processes mapped?
<--- Score

99. Scope of sensitive information?
<--- Score

100. What baselines are required to be defined and managed?
<--- Score

101. Has a high-level 'as is' process map been completed, verified and validated?
<--- Score

102. What are the Roles and Responsibilities for each team member and its leadership? Where is this documented?
<--- Score

103. How did the Incident and Crisis Management manager receive input to the development of a Incident and Crisis Management improvement plan and the estimated completion dates/times of each activity?
<--- Score

104. How often are the team meetings?

<--- Score

105. Is it clearly defined in and to your organization what you do?
<--- Score

106. What gets examined?
<--- Score

107. Is outside expert assistance required?
<--- Score

108. Is there regularly 100% attendance at the team meetings? If not, have appointed substitutes attended to preserve cross-functionality and full representation?
<--- Score

109. How would you define Incident and Crisis Management leadership?
<--- Score

110. How do you keep key subject matter experts in the loop?
<--- Score

111. Is there a completed, verified, and validated high-level 'as is' (not 'should be' or 'could be') stakeholder process map?
<--- Score

112. Has anyone else (internal or external to the group) attempted to solve this problem or a similar one before? If so, what knowledge can be leveraged from these previous efforts?
<--- Score

113. What specifically is the problem? Where does it occur? When does it occur? What is its extent?
<--- Score

114. How is the team tracking and documenting its work?
<--- Score

115. How was the 'as is' process map developed, reviewed, verified and validated?
<--- Score

116. How will the Incident and Crisis Management team and the group measure complete success of Incident and Crisis Management?
<--- Score

117. What sort of initial information to gather?
<--- Score

118. What is the context?
<--- Score

119. What is in scope?
<--- Score

120. Is the Incident and Crisis Management scope complete and appropriately sized?
<--- Score

121. What constraints exist that might impact the team?
<--- Score

122. Is the scope of Incident and Crisis Management

defined?
<--- Score

123. Are approval levels defined for contracts and supplements to contracts?
<--- Score

124. Has your scope been defined?
<--- Score

125. Are team charters developed?
<--- Score

126. Are the Incident and Crisis Management requirements complete?
<--- Score

127. Is the team adequately staffed with the desired cross-functionality? If not, what additional resources are available to the team?
<--- Score

128. Has everyone on the team, including the team leaders, been properly trained?
<--- Score

129. What is the scope of the Incident and Crisis Management work?
<--- Score

130. Has/have the customer(s) been identified?
<--- Score

131. Are improvement team members fully trained on Incident and Crisis Management?
<--- Score

132. Has a team charter been developed and communicated?
<--- Score

133. When is the estimated completion date?
<--- Score

134. Are task requirements clearly defined?
<--- Score

135. How are consistent Incident and Crisis Management definitions important?
<--- Score

Add up total points for this section:
_____ = Total points for this section

Divided by: _____ (number of statements answered) = _____
Average score for this section

Transfer your score to the Incident and Crisis Management Index at the beginning of the Self-Assessment.

CRITERION #3: MEASURE:

INTENT: Gather the correct data. Measure the current performance and evolution of the situation.

In my belief, the answer to this question is clearly defined:

5 Strongly Agree

4 Agree

3 Neutral

2 Disagree

1 Strongly Disagree

1. How can you reduce the costs of obtaining inputs?
<--- Score

2. What causes investor action?
<--- Score

3. What are the costs and benefits?
<--- Score

4. How do you focus on what is right -not who is right?
<--- Score

5. Is it possible to estimate the impact of unanticipated complexity such as wrong or failed assumptions, feedback, etcetera on proposed reforms?
<--- Score

6. Have design-to-cost goals been established?
<--- Score

7. What are the costs?
<--- Score

8. What are the types and number of measures to use?
<--- Score

9. Why do the measurements/indicators matter?
<--- Score

10. What disadvantage does this cause for the user?
<--- Score

11. How will the Incident and Crisis Management data be analyzed?
<--- Score

12. What are allowable costs?
<--- Score

13. How are measurements made?
<--- Score

14. Is the scope of Incident and Crisis Management

cost analysis cost-effective?
<--- Score

15. What potential environmental factors impact the Incident and Crisis Management effort?
<--- Score

16. Among the Incident and Crisis Management product and service cost to be estimated, which is considered hardest to estimate?
<--- Score

17. What would be a real cause for concern?
<--- Score

18. How do you verify performance?
<--- Score

19. What measurements are being captured?
<--- Score

20. What causes mismanagement?
<--- Score

21. Which Incident and Crisis Management impacts are significant?
<--- Score

22. When should you bother with diagrams?
<--- Score

23. What is your Incident and Crisis Management quality cost segregation study?
<--- Score

24. How can you measure the performance?

<--- Score

25. What are hidden Incident and Crisis Management quality costs?
<--- Score

26. What are your primary costs, revenues, assets?
<--- Score

27. Who should receive measurement reports?
<--- Score

28. What does your operating model cost?
<--- Score

29. The approach of traditional Incident and Crisis Management works for detail complexity but is focused on a systematic approach rather than an understanding of the nature of systems themselves, what approach will permit your organization to deal with the kind of unpredictable emergent behaviors that dynamic complexity can introduce?
<--- Score

30. Do you effectively measure and reward individual and team performance?
<--- Score

31. How frequently do you verify your Incident and Crisis Management strategy?
<--- Score

32. What are you verifying?
<--- Score

33. What details are required of the Incident and Crisis

Management cost structure?
<--- Score

34. Are there any easy-to-implement alternatives to Incident and Crisis Management? Sometimes other solutions are available that do not require the cost implications of a full-blown project?
<--- Score

35. What are the costs of delaying Incident and Crisis Management action?
<--- Score

36. What are the Incident and Crisis Management key cost drivers?
<--- Score

37. What are the costs of reform?
<--- Score

38. What evidence is there and what is measured?
<--- Score

39. How will measures be used to manage and adapt?
<--- Score

40. What can be used to verify compliance?
<--- Score

41. Are there competing Incident and Crisis Management priorities?
<--- Score

42. How can you measure Incident and Crisis Management in a systematic way?
<--- Score

43. What are your operating costs?
<--- Score

44. Are indirect costs charged to the Incident and Crisis Management program?
<--- Score

45. How will success or failure be measured?
<--- Score

46. What relevant entities could be measured?
<--- Score

47. Do you verify that corrective actions were taken?
<--- Score

48. Are actual costs in line with budgeted costs?
<--- Score

49. What are the uncertainties surrounding estimates of impact?
<--- Score

50. Does a Incident and Crisis Management quantification method exist?
<--- Score

51. Has a cost center been established?
<--- Score

52. How much does it cost?
<--- Score

53. Was a life-cycle cost analysis performed?
<--- Score

54. Do you have a flow diagram of what happens?
<--- Score

55. How sensitive must the Incident and Crisis Management strategy be to cost?
<--- Score

56. What are predictive Incident and Crisis Management analytics?
<--- Score

57. Was a business case (cost/benefit) developed?
<--- Score

58. Why a Incident and Crisis Management focus?
<--- Score

59. What is an unallowable cost?
<--- Score

60. What would it cost to replace your technology?
<--- Score

61. What tests verify requirements?
<--- Score

62. What causes extra work or rework?
<--- Score

63. Do the benefits outweigh the costs?
<--- Score

64. How will costs be allocated?
<--- Score

65. What is the Incident and Crisis Management business impact?
<--- Score

66. What is the total cost related to deploying Incident and Crisis Management, including any consulting or professional services?
<--- Score

67. Are the Incident and Crisis Management benefits worth its costs?
<--- Score

68. Are you taking your company in the direction of better and revenue or cheaper and cost?
<--- Score

69. What causes innovation to fail or succeed in your organization?
<--- Score

70. Do you have an issue in getting priority?
<--- Score

71. How do you measure variability?
<--- Score

72. What are the strategic priorities for this year?
<--- Score

73. When are costs are incurred?
<--- Score

74. Do you aggressively reward and promote the people who have the biggest impact on creating excellent Incident and Crisis Management services/

products?
<--- Score

75. Where can you go to verify the info?
<--- Score

76. How do you verify Incident and Crisis Management completeness and accuracy?
<--- Score

77. Have you made assumptions about the shape of the future, particularly its impact on your customers and competitors?
<--- Score

78. What is the total fixed cost?
<--- Score

79. How is performance measured?
<--- Score

80. How are you verifying it?
<--- Score

81. What is your decision requirements diagram?
<--- Score

82. What could cause delays in the schedule?
<--- Score

83. How is progress measured?
<--- Score

84. What drives O&M cost?
<--- Score

85. Have the it and business process root causes been identified?

<--- Score

86. What do you measure and why?

<--- Score

87. How do you verify the Incident and Crisis Management requirements quality?

<--- Score

88. At what cost?

<--- Score

89. How do you measure efficient delivery of Incident and Crisis Management services?

<--- Score

90. How to cause the change?

<--- Score

91. Are you aware of what could cause a problem?

<--- Score

92. How long to keep data and how to manage retention costs?

<--- Score

93. Which measures and indicators matter?

<--- Score

94. What are your customers expectations and measures?

<--- Score

95. Are you able to realize any cost savings?

<--- Score

96. What are the operational costs after Incident and Crisis Management deployment?
<--- Score

97. What is the cost of rework?
<--- Score

98. Are missed Incident and Crisis Management opportunities costing your organization money?
<--- Score

99. What is your cost benefit analysis?
<--- Score

100. How will effects be measured?
<--- Score

101. How do you verify and validate the Incident and Crisis Management data?
<--- Score

102. Where is the cost?
<--- Score

103. What are the Incident and Crisis Management investment costs?
<--- Score

104. Did you tackle the cause or the symptom?
<--- Score

105. How can a Incident and Crisis Management test verify your ideas or assumptions?
<--- Score

106. How will you measure success?
<--- Score

107. How frequently do you track Incident and Crisis Management measures?
<--- Score

108. What is measured? Why?
<--- Score

109. Is there an opportunity to verify requirements?
<--- Score

110. What does a Test Case verify?
<--- Score

111. How will you measure your Incident and Crisis Management effectiveness?
<--- Score

112. Why do you expend time and effort to implement measurement, for whom?
<--- Score

113. Is the cost worth the Incident and Crisis Management effort ?
<--- Score

114. How do you verify the authenticity of the data and information used?
<--- Score

115. Is the solution cost-effective?
<--- Score

116. Are supply costs steady or fluctuating?
<--- Score

117. What is the cause of any Incident and Crisis Management gaps?
<--- Score

118. Are there measurements based on task performance?
<--- Score

119. How is the value delivered by Incident and Crisis Management being measured?
<--- Score

120. How do your measurements capture actionable Incident and Crisis Management information for use in exceeding your customers expectations and securing your customers engagement?
<--- Score

121. What users will be impacted?
<--- Score

122. What does losing customers cost your organization?
<--- Score

123. How do you prevent mis-estimating cost?
<--- Score

124. What do people want to verify?
<--- Score

125. Will Incident and Crisis Management have an impact on current business continuity, disaster

recovery processes and/or infrastructure?
<--- Score

126. Does management have the right priorities among projects?
<--- Score

127. How does cost-to-serve analysis help?
<--- Score

128. Do you have any cost Incident and Crisis Management limitation requirements?
<--- Score

129. How can you manage cost down?
<--- Score

130. Are Incident and Crisis Management vulnerabilities categorized and prioritized?
<--- Score

131. What does verifying compliance entail?
<--- Score

132. What are your key Incident and Crisis Management organizational performance measures, including key short and longer-term financial measures?
<--- Score

133. What methods are feasible and acceptable to estimate the impact of reforms?
<--- Score

134. Are the measurements objective?
<--- Score

135. How will your organization measure success?
<--- Score

136. Are the units of measure consistent?
<--- Score

137. How do you control the overall costs of your work processes?
<--- Score

Add up total points for this section:
_ _ _ _ _ = Total points for this section

Divided by: _ _ _ _ _ _ (number of statements answered) = _ _ _ _ _ _
Average score for this section

Transfer your score to the Incident and Crisis Management Index at the beginning of the Self-Assessment.

CRITERION #4: ANALYZE:

INTENT: Analyze causes, assumptions and hypotheses.

In my belief, the answer to this question is clearly defined:

5 Strongly Agree

4 Agree

3 Neutral

2 Disagree

1 Strongly Disagree

1. What systems/processes must you excel at?
<--- Score

2. Are all staff in core Incident and Crisis Management subjects Highly Qualified?
<--- Score

3. How many input/output points does it require?
<--- Score

4. Where is the data coming from to measure compliance?
<--- Score

5. What are your key performance measures or indicators and in-process measures for the control and improvement of your Incident and Crisis Management processes?
<--- Score

6. How is the Incident and Crisis Management Value Stream Mapping managed?
<--- Score

7. Is there an established change management process?
<--- Score

8. Is the gap/opportunity displayed and communicated in financial terms?
<--- Score

9. What is the process and timeline?
<--- Score

10. Is the suppliers process defined and controlled?
<--- Score

11. How do you measure the operational performance of your key work systems and processes, including productivity, cycle time, and other appropriate measures of process effectiveness, efficiency, and innovation?
<--- Score

12. Do you understand your management processes

today?
<--- Score

13. What are your outputs?
<--- Score

14. Has data output been validated?
<--- Score

15. Think about some of the processes you undertake within your organization, which do you own?
<--- Score

16. How do mission and objectives affect the Incident and Crisis Management processes of your organization?
<--- Score

17. What are the Incident and Crisis Management design outputs?
<--- Score

18. Where can you get qualified talent today?
<--- Score

19. Who is involved in the management review process?
<--- Score

20. Do you have the authority to produce the output?
<--- Score

21. What are the processes for audit reporting and management?
<--- Score

22. What are the best opportunities for value improvement?
<--- Score

23. How can risk management be tied procedurally to process elements?
<--- Score

24. What conclusions were drawn from the team's data collection and analysis? How did the team reach these conclusions?
<--- Score

25. Who qualifies to gain access to data?
<--- Score

26. Were Pareto charts (or similar) used to portray the 'heavy hitters' (or key sources of variation)?
<--- Score

27. What Incident and Crisis Management data will be collected?
<--- Score

28. Was a cause-and-effect diagram used to explore the different types of causes (or sources of variation)?
<--- Score

29. What Incident and Crisis Management data do you gather or use now?
<--- Score

30. What training and qualifications will you need?
<--- Score

31. Has an output goal been set?

<--- Score

32. What resources go in to get the desired output?
<--- Score

33. What data do you need to collect?
<--- Score

34. How was the detailed process map generated, verified, and validated?
<--- Score

35. Have you defined which data is gathered how?
<--- Score

36. Is the final output clearly identified?
<--- Score

37. What qualifications are necessary?
<--- Score

38. What tools were used to generate the list of possible causes?
<--- Score

39. How is Incident and Crisis Management data gathered?
<--- Score

40. Are gaps between current performance and the goal performance identified?
<--- Score

41. Were there any improvement opportunities identified from the process analysis?
<--- Score

42. How will the data be checked for quality?
<--- Score

43. What are the revised rough estimates of the financial savings/opportunity for Incident and Crisis Management improvements?
<--- Score

44. What are your best practices for minimizing Incident and Crisis Management project risk, while demonstrating incremental value and quick wins throughout the Incident and Crisis Management project lifecycle?
<--- Score

45. What will drive Incident and Crisis Management change?
<--- Score

46. What are the necessary qualifications?
<--- Score

47. Are your outputs consistent?
<--- Score

48. Should you invest in industry-recognized qualifications?
<--- Score

49. What quality tools were used to get through the analyze phase?
<--- Score

50. Is the required Incident and Crisis Management data gathered?

<--- Score

51. Is critical processes needed resources?
<--- Score

52. Was a detailed process map created to amplify critical steps of the 'as is' stakeholder process?
<--- Score

53. How do your work systems and key work processes relate to and capitalize on your core competencies?
<--- Score

54. Did any additional data need to be collected?
<--- Score

55. What were the crucial 'moments of truth' on the process map?
<--- Score

56. What qualifications do Incident and Crisis Management leaders need?
<--- Score

57. Is there a strict change management process?
<--- Score

58. What is the cost of poor quality as supported by the team's analysis?
<--- Score

59. What is the oversight process?
<--- Score

60. Identify an operational issue in your organization,

for example, could a particular task be done more quickly or more efficiently by Incident and Crisis Management?
<--- Score

61. Were any designed experiments used to generate additional insight into the data analysis?
<--- Score

62. What is your organizations process which leads to recognition of value generation?
<--- Score

63. Which Incident and Crisis Management data should be retained?
<--- Score

64. Is there any way to speed up the process?
<--- Score

65. Do your leaders quickly bounce back from setbacks?
<--- Score

66. A compounding model resolution with available relevant data can often provide insight towards a solution methodology; which Incident and Crisis Management models, tools and techniques are necessary?
<--- Score

67. What kind of crime could a potential new hire have committed that would not only not disqualify him/her from being hired by your organization, but would actually indicate that he/she might be a particularly good fit?

<--- Score

68. What did the team gain from developing a sub-process map?
<--- Score

69. How do you define collaboration and team output?
<--- Score

70. What is the Value Stream Mapping?
<--- Score

71. How is data used for program management and improvement?
<--- Score

72. What internal processes need improvement?
<--- Score

73. Have the problem and goal statements been updated to reflect the additional knowledge gained from the analyze phase?
<--- Score

74. What is your organizations system for selecting qualified vendors?
<--- Score

75. Do staff qualifications match your project?
<--- Score

76. How will the change process be managed?
<--- Score

77. Who will facilitate the team and process?

<--- Score

78. What is the output?
<--- Score

79. What Incident and Crisis Management metrics are outputs of the process?
<--- Score

80. What controls do you have in place to protect data?
<--- Score

81. What information qualified as important?
<--- Score

82. What Incident and Crisis Management data should be managed?
<--- Score

83. What is the Incident and Crisis Management Driver?
<--- Score

84. How do you identify specific Incident and Crisis Management investment opportunities and emerging trends?
<--- Score

85. Do quality systems drive continuous improvement?
<--- Score

86. What other organizational variables, such as reward systems or communication systems, affect the performance of this Incident and Crisis Management

process?
<--- Score

87. An organizationally feasible system request is one that considers the mission, goals and objectives of the organization, key questions are: is the Incident and Crisis Management solution request practical and will it solve a problem or take advantage of an opportunity to achieve company goals?
<--- Score

88. What qualifications and skills do you need?
<--- Score

89. What methods do you use to gather Incident and Crisis Management data?
<--- Score

90. What other jobs or tasks affect the performance of the steps in the Incident and Crisis Management process?
<--- Score

91. Are there significant milestones in the recovery process that could be used for publicity?
<--- Score

92. Is the Incident and Crisis Management process severely broken such that a re-design is necessary?
<--- Score

93. Do several people in different organizational units assist with the Incident and Crisis Management process?
<--- Score

94. What are the Incident and Crisis Management business drivers?
<--- Score

95. Is the performance gap determined?
<--- Score

96. How does the organization define, manage, and improve its Incident and Crisis Management processes?
<--- Score

97. What successful thing are you doing today that may be blinding you to new growth opportunities?
<--- Score

98. Who will gather what data?
<--- Score

99. How is the data gathered?
<--- Score

100. How will corresponding data be collected?
<--- Score

101. What Incident and Crisis Management data should be collected?
<--- Score

102. When should a process be art not science?
<--- Score

103. How has the Incident and Crisis Management data been gathered?
<--- Score

104. What tools were used to narrow the list of possible causes?
<--- Score

105. What are your current levels and trends in key Incident and Crisis Management measures or indicators of product and process performance that are important to and directly serve your customers?
<--- Score

106. What were the financial benefits resulting from any 'ground fruit or low-hanging fruit' (quick fixes)?
<--- Score

107. Are you missing Incident and Crisis Management opportunities?
<--- Score

108. Is data and process analysis, root cause analysis and quantifying the gap/opportunity in place?
<--- Score

109. How difficult is it to qualify what Incident and Crisis Management ROI is?
<--- Score

110. How often will data be collected for measures?
<--- Score

111. What, related to, Incident and Crisis Management processes does your organization outsource?
<--- Score

112. Have any additional benefits been identified that will result from closing all or most of the gaps?
<--- Score

113. What are your current levels and trends in key measures or indicators of Incident and Crisis Management product and process performance that are important to and directly serve your customers? How do these results compare with the performance of your competitors and other organizations with similar offerings?
<--- Score

114. What does the data say about the performance of the stakeholder process?
<--- Score

115. How do you implement and manage your work processes to ensure that they meet design requirements?
<--- Score

116. Do your employees have the opportunity to do what they do best everyday?
<--- Score

117. Did any value-added analysis or 'lean thinking' take place to identify some of the gaps shown on the 'as is' process map?
<--- Score

118. What are your Incident and Crisis Management processes?
<--- Score

119. Who owns what data?
<--- Score

120. Is pre-qualification of suppliers carried out?

<--- Score

121. How do you ensure that the Incident and Crisis Management opportunity is realistic?
<--- Score

122. Think about the functions involved in your Incident and Crisis Management project, what processes flow from these functions?
<--- Score

123. What qualifies as competition?
<--- Score

124. What data is gathered?
<--- Score

125. Are all team members qualified for all tasks?
<--- Score

126. What are the disruptive Incident and Crisis Management technologies that enable your organization to radically change your business processes?
<--- Score

127. What do you need to qualify?
<--- Score

128. What process should you select for improvement?
<--- Score

Add up total points for this section:
_____ = Total points for this section

Divided by: _____ (number of statements answered) = _____
Average score for this section

Transfer your score to the Incident and Crisis Management Index at the beginning of the Self-Assessment.

CRITERION #5: IMPROVE:

INTENT: Develop a practical solution. Innovate, establish and test the solution and to measure the results.

In my belief, the answer to this question is clearly defined:

5 Strongly Agree

4 Agree

3 Neutral

2 Disagree

1 Strongly Disagree

1. How can you better manage risk?
<--- Score

2. What assumptions are made about the solution and approach?
<--- Score

3. Incident and Crisis Management risk decisions: whose call Is It?

<--- Score

4. Is there any other Incident and Crisis Management solution?
<--- Score

5. What Incident and Crisis Management improvements can be made?
<--- Score

6. How do you define the solutions' scope?
<--- Score

7. What to do with the results or outcomes of measurements?
<--- Score

8. What current systems have to be understood and/or changed?
<--- Score

9. How are Incident and Crisis Management risks managed?
<--- Score

10. What do you want to improve?
<--- Score

11. What tools were used to evaluate the potential solutions?
<--- Score

12. What tools were used to tap into the creativity and encourage 'outside the box' thinking?
<--- Score

13. Risk Identification: What are the possible risk events your organization faces in relation to Incident and Crisis Management?
<--- Score

14. Is there a high likelihood that any recommendations will achieve their intended results?
<--- Score

15. Are events managed to resolution?
<--- Score

16. Which of the recognised risks out of all risks can be most likely transferred?
<--- Score

17. How do you manage and improve your Incident and Crisis Management work systems to deliver customer value and achieve organizational success and sustainability?
<--- Score

18. Will the controls trigger any other risks?
<--- Score

19. How do you measure risk?
<--- Score

20. Would you develop a Incident and Crisis Management Communication Strategy?
<--- Score

21. What are the concrete Incident and Crisis Management results?
<--- Score

22. How risky is your organization?
<--- Score

23. Can you identify any significant risks or exposures to Incident and Crisis Management third- parties (vendors, service providers, alliance partners etc) that concern you?
<--- Score

24. Risk factors: what are the characteristics of Incident and Crisis Management that make it risky?
<--- Score

25. How will you measure the results?
<--- Score

26. Was a pilot designed for the proposed solution(s)?
<--- Score

27. Who are the people involved in developing and implementing Incident and Crisis Management?
<--- Score

28. What practices helps your organization to develop its capacity to recognize patterns?
<--- Score

29. Is the Incident and Crisis Management risk managed?
<--- Score

30. What does the 'should be' process map/design look like?
<--- Score

31. Is the solution technically practical?

<--- Score

32. What is Incident and Crisis Management risk?
<--- Score

33. How scalable is your Incident and Crisis Management solution?
<--- Score

34. Was a Incident and Crisis Management charter developed?
<--- Score

35. Is any Incident and Crisis Management documentation required?
<--- Score

36. Who are the Incident and Crisis Management decision makers?
<--- Score

37. How will you know that a change is an improvement?
<--- Score

38. How is continuous improvement applied to risk management?
<--- Score

39. Who will be using the results of the measurement activities?
<--- Score

40. At what point will vulnerability assessments be performed once Incident and Crisis Management is put into production (e.g., ongoing Risk Management

after implementation)?
<--- Score

41. How do you improve Incident and Crisis Management service perception, and satisfaction?
<--- Score

42. What tools do you use once you have decided on a Incident and Crisis Management strategy and more importantly how do you choose?
<--- Score

43. Do those selected for the Incident and Crisis Management team have a good general understanding of what Incident and Crisis Management is all about?
<--- Score

44. What were the criteria for evaluating a Incident and Crisis Management pilot?
<--- Score

45. Where do you need Incident and Crisis Management improvement?
<--- Score

46. What is the involvement in authorities in decision making, especially to restart operations?
<--- Score

47. Have you achieved Incident and Crisis Management improvements?
<--- Score

48. What communications are necessary to support the implementation of the solution?

<--- Score

49. Are all participants accounted for and aware of risk?
<--- Score

50. How will you know that you have improved?
<--- Score

51. What resources are required for the improvement efforts?
<--- Score

52. Risk events: what are the things that could go wrong?
<--- Score

53. What should a proof of concept or pilot accomplish?
<--- Score

54. Who are the key stakeholders for the Incident and Crisis Management evaluation?
<--- Score

55. How significant is the improvement in the eyes of the end user?
<--- Score

56. How do you keep improving Incident and Crisis Management?
<--- Score

57. Which Incident and Crisis Management solution is appropriate?
<--- Score

58. To what extent does management recognize Incident and Crisis Management as a tool to increase the results?
<--- Score

59. How will you know when its improved?
<--- Score

60. How do you improve your likelihood of success ?
<--- Score

61. Where did elected officials and organization heads meet to make policy decisions?
<--- Score

62. Does a good decision guarantee a good outcome?
<--- Score

63. What improvements have been achieved?
<--- Score

64. Why improve in the first place?
<--- Score

65. Is there a small-scale pilot for proposed improvement(s)? What conclusions were drawn from the outcomes of a pilot?
<--- Score

66. Were any criteria developed to assist the team in testing and evaluating potential solutions?
<--- Score

67. Do you cover the five essential competencies: Communication, Collaboration,Innovation,

Adaptability, and Leadership that improve an organizations ability to leverage the new Incident and Crisis Management in a volatile global economy?
<--- Score

68. What is the implementation plan?
<--- Score

69. If you could go back in time five years, what decision would you make differently? What is your best guess as to what decision you're making today you might regret five years from now?
<--- Score

70. What alternative responses are available to manage risk?
<--- Score

71. Is supporting Incident and Crisis Management documentation required?
<--- Score

72. For estimation problems, how do you develop an estimation statement?
<--- Score

73. Who are the Incident and Crisis Management decision-makers?
<--- Score

74. Are the risks fully understood, reasonable and manageable?
<--- Score

75. Do you combine technical expertise with business knowledge and Incident and Crisis Management Key

topics include lifecycles, development approaches, requirements and how to make a business case?
<--- Score

76. What are the Incident and Crisis Management security risks?
<--- Score

77. Who do you report Incident and Crisis Management results to?
<--- Score

78. Is Incident and Crisis Management documentation maintained?
<--- Score

79. Do you have the optimal project management team structure?
<--- Score

80. Can you integrate quality management and risk management?
<--- Score

81. What types of damage occurred as a result of the event?
<--- Score

82. How do you go about comparing Incident and Crisis Management approaches/solutions?
<--- Score

83. How do you improve productivity?
<--- Score

84. What were the underlying assumptions on the

cost-benefit analysis?
<--- Score

85. What is Incident and Crisis Management's impact on utilizing the best solution(s)?
<--- Score

86. How does your organization evaluate strategic Incident and Crisis Management success?
<--- Score

87. What lessons, if any, from a pilot were incorporated into the design of the full-scale solution?
<--- Score

88. What tools were most useful during the improve phase?
<--- Score

89. Who controls key decisions that will be made?
<--- Score

90. How will you recognize and celebrate results?
<--- Score

91. How does the team improve its work?
<--- Score

92. Are procedures documented for managing Incident and Crisis Management risks?
<--- Score

93. Who will be responsible for making the decisions to include or exclude requested changes once Incident and Crisis Management is underway?
<--- Score

94. What can you do to improve?
<--- Score

95. How do you link measurement and risk?
<--- Score

96. Who should make the Incident and Crisis Management decisions?
<--- Score

97. How do you manage Incident and Crisis Management risk?
<--- Score

98. How do you decide how much to remunerate an employee?
<--- Score

99. What error proofing will be done to address some of the discrepancies observed in the 'as is' process?
<--- Score

100. What criteria will you use to assess your Incident and Crisis Management risks?
<--- Score

101. How are policy decisions made and where?
<--- Score

102. Who makes the Incident and Crisis Management decisions in your organization?
<--- Score

103. What are the affordable Incident and Crisis Management risks?

<--- Score

104. How can you improve Incident and Crisis Management?
<--- Score

105. Are risk management tasks balanced centrally and locally?
<--- Score

106. How do you measure progress and evaluate training effectiveness?
<--- Score

107. In the past few months, what is the smallest change you have made that has had the biggest positive result? What was it about that small change that produced the large return?
<--- Score

108. What actually has to improve and by how much?
<--- Score

109. For decision problems, how do you develop a decision statement?
<--- Score

110. Who manages supplier risk management in your organization?
<--- Score

111. Explorations of the frontiers of Incident and Crisis Management will help you build influence, improve Incident and Crisis Management, optimize decision making, and sustain change, what is your approach?
<--- Score

112. Is risk periodically assessed?
<--- Score

113. Are the key business and technology risks being managed?
<--- Score

114. Are the most efficient solutions problem-specific?
<--- Score

115. How is knowledge sharing about risk management improved?
<--- Score

116. Can the solution be designed and implemented within an acceptable time period?
<--- Score

117. What is the Incident and Crisis Management's sustainability risk?
<--- Score

118. Who manages Incident and Crisis Management risk?
<--- Score

119. Is the scope clearly documented?
<--- Score

120. How do the Incident and Crisis Management results compare with the performance of your competitors and other organizations with similar offerings?
<--- Score

121. Have you identified breakpoints and/or risk tolerances that will trigger broad consideration of a potential need for intervention or modification of strategy?

<--- Score

122. What is the team's contingency plan for potential problems occurring in implementation?

<--- Score

123. Is the measure of success for Incident and Crisis Management understandable to a variety of people?

<--- Score

124. What went well, what should change, what can improve?

<--- Score

125. Does the goal represent a desired result that can be measured?

<--- Score

126. Is the Incident and Crisis Management solution sustainable?

<--- Score

127. When you map the key players in your own work and the types/domains of relationships with them, which relationships do you find easy and which challenging, and why?

<--- Score

128. What strategies for Incident and Crisis Management improvement are successful?

<--- Score

129. What attendant changes will need to be made to ensure that the solution is successful?
<--- Score

130. Where do the Incident and Crisis Management decisions reside?
<--- Score

131. What area needs the greatest improvement?
<--- Score

132. Is the Incident and Crisis Management documentation thorough?
<--- Score

133. Who controls the risk?
<--- Score

134. Do you need to do a usability evaluation?
<--- Score

Add up total points for this section:
_____ = Total points for this section

Divided by: _____ (number of statements answered) = _____
Average score for this section

Transfer your score to the Incident and Crisis Management Index at the beginning of the Self-Assessment.

CRITERION #6: CONTROL:

INTENT: Implement the practical solution. Maintain the performance and correct possible complications.

In my belief, the answer to this question is clearly defined:

5 Strongly Agree

4 Agree

3 Neutral

2 Disagree

1 Strongly Disagree

1. Are you measuring, monitoring and predicting Incident and Crisis Management activities to optimize operations and profitability, and enhancing outcomes?
<--- Score

2. What do you measure to verify effectiveness gains?
<--- Score

3. What do your reports reflect?
<--- Score

4. What is your theory of human motivation, and how does your compensation plan fit with that view?
<--- Score

5. How do controls support value?
<--- Score

6. What other areas of the group might benefit from the Incident and Crisis Management team's improvements, knowledge, and learning?
<--- Score

7. How will new or emerging customer needs/requirements be checked/communicated to orient the process toward meeting the new specifications and continually reducing variation?
<--- Score

8. Will the team be available to assist members in planning investigations?
<--- Score

9. What are you attempting to measure/monitor?
<--- Score

10. Does the Incident and Crisis Management performance meet the customer's requirements?
<--- Score

11. Does a troubleshooting guide exist or is it needed?
<--- Score

12. Is there a recommended audit plan for routine

surveillance inspections of Incident and Crisis Management's gains?
<--- Score

13. Implementation Planning: is a pilot needed to test the changes before a full roll out occurs?
<--- Score

14. Do the viable solutions scale to future needs?
<--- Score

15. How widespread is its use?
<--- Score

16. Is there a documented and implemented monitoring plan?
<--- Score

17. Is there a standardized process?
<--- Score

18. Can you adapt and adjust to changing Incident and Crisis Management situations?
<--- Score

19. Did the person tell anyone of plans to be absent?
<--- Score

20. What Incident and Crisis Management standards are applicable?
<--- Score

21. Does job training on the documented procedures need to be part of the process team's education and training?

<--- Score

22. What are the performance and scale of the Incident and Crisis Management tools?
<--- Score

23. Act/Adjust: What Do you Need to Do Differently?
<--- Score

24. What is the recommended frequency of auditing?
<--- Score

25. Are operating procedures consistent?
<--- Score

26. How do you establish and deploy modified action plans if circumstances require a shift in plans and rapid execution of new plans?
<--- Score

27. In the case of a Incident and Crisis Management project, the criteria for the audit derive from implementation objectives, an audit of a Incident and Crisis Management project involves assessing whether the recommendations outlined for implementation have been met, can you track that any Incident and Crisis Management project is implemented as planned, and is it working?
<--- Score

28. Is there a Incident and Crisis Management Communication plan covering who needs to get what information when?
<--- Score

29. You may have created your quality measures at a

time when you lacked resources, technology wasn't up to the required standard, or low service levels were the industry norm. Have those circumstances changed?
<--- Score

30. Are documented procedures clear and easy to follow for the operators?
<--- Score

31. Has the improved process and its steps been standardized?
<--- Score

32. Are pertinent alerts monitored, analyzed and distributed to appropriate personnel?
<--- Score

33. How do your controls stack up?
<--- Score

34. Is a response plan established and deployed?
<--- Score

35. Has the Incident and Crisis Management value of standards been quantified?
<--- Score

36. Who will be in control?
<--- Score

37. What is the standard for acceptable Incident and Crisis Management performance?
<--- Score

38. Who is going to spread your message?

<--- Score

39. Are suggested corrective/restorative actions indicated on the response plan for known causes to problems that might surface?
<--- Score

40. Are there documented procedures?
<--- Score

41. What are your results for key measures or indicators of the accomplishment of your Incident and Crisis Management strategy and action plans, including building and strengthening core competencies?
<--- Score

42. What are the critical parameters to watch?
<--- Score

43. Are you periodically testing your plan and training your staff?
<--- Score

44. Who controls critical resources?
<--- Score

45. Is there a transfer of ownership and knowledge to process owner and process team tasked with the responsibilities.
<--- Score

46. How will report readings be checked to effectively monitor performance?
<--- Score

47. What quality tools were useful in the control phase?
<--- Score

48. Can support from partners be adjusted?
<--- Score

49. How do you plan on providing proper recognition and disclosure of supporting companies?
<--- Score

50. What should the next improvement project be that is related to Incident and Crisis Management?
<--- Score

51. What do you stand for--and what are you against?
<--- Score

52. What are the known security controls?
<--- Score

53. How will you measure your QA plan's effectiveness?
<--- Score

54. Does Incident and Crisis Management appropriately measure and monitor risk?
<--- Score

55. What key inputs and outputs are being measured on an ongoing basis?
<--- Score

56. Is reporting being used or needed?
<--- Score

57. Is the Incident and Crisis Management test/monitoring cost justified?
<--- Score

58. How likely is the current Incident and Crisis Management plan to come in on schedule or on budget?
<--- Score

59. How do you encourage people to take control and responsibility?
<--- Score

60. What are the key elements of your Incident and Crisis Management performance improvement system, including your evaluation, organizational learning, and innovation processes?
<--- Score

61. Are new process steps, standards, and documentation ingrained into normal operations?
<--- Score

62. How will input, process, and output variables be checked to detect for sub-optimal conditions?
<--- Score

63. How might the group capture best practices and lessons learned so as to leverage improvements?
<--- Score

64. How do you plan for the cost of succession?
<--- Score

65. Are the planned controls working?
<--- Score

66. What adjustments to the strategies are needed?
<--- Score

67. What can you control?
<--- Score

68. What should you measure to verify efficiency gains?
<--- Score

69. Have new or revised work instructions resulted?
<--- Score

70. Who has control over resources?
<--- Score

71. How can you best use all of your knowledge repositories to enhance learning and sharing?
<--- Score

72. What are customers monitoring?
<--- Score

73. Against what alternative is success being measured?
<--- Score

74. Who is the Incident and Crisis Management process owner?
<--- Score

75. What is the control/monitoring plan?
<--- Score

76. Is a response plan in place for when the input,

process, or output measures indicate an 'out-of-control' condition?
<--- Score

77. Who is monitoring media coverage?
<--- Score

78. Is knowledge gained on process shared and institutionalized?
<--- Score

79. What other systems, operations, processes, and infrastructures (hiring practices, staffing, training, incentives/rewards, metrics/dashboards/scorecards, etc.) need updates, additions, changes, or deletions in order to facilitate knowledge transfer and improvements?
<--- Score

80. How do senior leaders actions reflect a commitment to the organizations Incident and Crisis Management values?
<--- Score

81. How do you monitor usage and cost?
<--- Score

82. How widespread is the media coverage?
<--- Score

83. Does the response plan contain a definite closed loop continual improvement scheme (e.g., plan-do-check-act)?
<--- Score

84. Is there a control plan in place for sustaining

improvements (short and long-term)?
<--- Score

85. How will the process owner and team be able to hold the gains?
<--- Score

86. How will Incident and Crisis Management decisions be made and monitored?
<--- Score

87. How do you spread information?
<--- Score

88. Is new knowledge gained imbedded in the response plan?
<--- Score

89. Will any special training be provided for results interpretation?
<--- Score

90. Is there documentation that will support the successful operation of the improvement?
<--- Score

91. How will the process owner verify improvement in present and future sigma levels, process capabilities?
<--- Score

92. How will the day-to-day responsibilities for monitoring and continual improvement be transferred from the improvement team to the process owner?
<--- Score

93. What is your plan to assess your security risks?
<--- Score

94. How do you select, collect, align, and integrate Incident and Crisis Management data and information for tracking daily operations and overall organizational performance, including progress relative to strategic objectives and action plans?
<--- Score

95. Are the planned controls in place?
<--- Score

96. Do you monitor the effectiveness of your Incident and Crisis Management activities?
<--- Score

97. Do you monitor the Incident and Crisis Management decisions made and fine tune them as they evolve?
<--- Score

98. Will your goals reflect your program budget?
<--- Score

99. What should be learned from the crisis?
<--- Score

Add up total points for this section:
_____ = Total points for this section

Divided by: _____ (number of statements answered) = _____
Average score for this section

Transfer your score to the Incident

and Crisis Management Index at the beginning of the Self-Assessment.

CRITERION #7: SUSTAIN:

INTENT: Retain the benefits.

In my belief, the answer to this question is clearly defined:

5 Strongly Agree

4 Agree

3 Neutral

2 Disagree

1 Strongly Disagree

1. Has the participant been given legal representation?
<--- Score

2. How can you become more high-tech but still be high touch?
<--- Score

3. Is your strategy driving your strategy? Or is the way in which you allocate resources driving your strategy?
<--- Score

4. What suggestions do you have to assist your recovery efforts?

<--- Score

5. Is there any existing Incident and Crisis Management governance structure?

<--- Score

6. Why should you adopt a Incident and Crisis Management framework?

<--- Score

7. Have benefits been optimized with all key stakeholders?

<--- Score

8. How do you assess the Incident and Crisis Management pitfalls that are inherent in implementing it?

<--- Score

9. How do you make it meaningful in connecting Incident and Crisis Management with what users do day-to-day?

<--- Score

10. Is there any reason to believe the opposite of my current belief?

<--- Score

11. What is the funding source for this project?

<--- Score

12. What actions must you complete to achieve the objectives?

<--- Score

13. Who do we want your customers to become?
<--- Score

14. What is the nature of the crisis?
<--- Score

15. What is a feasible sequencing of reform initiatives over time?
<--- Score

16. Ask yourself: how would you do this work if you only had one staff member to do it?
<--- Score

17. Who will provide the final approval of Incident and Crisis Management deliverables?
<--- Score

18. What is your formula for success in Incident and Crisis Management ?
<--- Score

19. If no one would ever find out about your accomplishments, how would you lead differently?
<--- Score

20. Do you think Incident and Crisis Management accomplishes the goals you expect it to accomplish?
<--- Score

21. Is a Incident and Crisis Management team work effort in place?
<--- Score

22. Will there be any necessary staff changes (redundancies or new hires)?
<--- Score

23. What trouble can you get into?
<--- Score

24. Do you have mobile numbers for all the key people?
<--- Score

25. Which functions and people interact with the supplier and or customer?
<--- Score

26. What are the challenges?
<--- Score

27. Are there any activities that you can take off your to do list?
<--- Score

28. Who leads your incident and crisis management program?
<--- Score

29. How can you incorporate support to ensure safe and effective use of Incident and Crisis Management into the services that you provide?
<--- Score

30. Can you do all this work?
<--- Score

31. If you had to leave your organization for a year and the only communication you could have with

employees/colleagues was a single paragraph, what would you write?

<--- Score

32. Are assumptions made in Incident and Crisis Management stated explicitly?

<--- Score

33. What is the nature and potential duration of the crisis?

<--- Score

34. Are new benefits received and understood?

<--- Score

35. What organization has made arrest / detention?

<--- Score

36. What are internal and external Incident and Crisis Management relations?

<--- Score

37. How will you insure seamless interoperability of Incident and Crisis Management moving forward?

<--- Score

38. Will it be accepted by users?

<--- Score

39. How do you proactively clarify deliverables and Incident and Crisis Management quality expectations?

<--- Score

40. What threat is Incident and Crisis Management addressing?

<--- Score

41. How does Incident and Crisis Management integrate with other stakeholder initiatives?
<--- Score

42. What is your question? Why?
<--- Score

43. Who is on the team?
<--- Score

44. Did your employees make progress today?
<--- Score

45. How will you know if the mitigation efforts have been successful?
<--- Score

46. What are the essentials of internal Incident and Crisis Management management?
<--- Score

47. Are the assumptions believable and achievable?
<--- Score

48. Is the group directly threatened or in imminent danger?
<--- Score

49. If there were zero limitations, what would you do differently?
<--- Score

50. How do you manage Incident and Crisis Management Knowledge Management (KM)?

<--- Score

51. Marketing budgets are tighter, consumers are more skeptical, and social media has changed forever the way we talk about Incident and Crisis Management, how do you gain traction?
<--- Score

52. If you were responsible for initiating and implementing major changes in your organization, what steps might you take to ensure acceptance of those changes?
<--- Score

53. What are the barriers to increased Incident and Crisis Management production?
<--- Score

54. What is the recommended frequency of auditing?
<--- Score

55. How do you foster innovation?
<--- Score

56. How do you deal with Incident and Crisis Management changes?
<--- Score

57. Why an integrated emergency management system?
<--- Score

58. What are strategies for increasing support and reducing opposition?
<--- Score

59. Are there serious health concerns if participants share rooms?
<--- Score

60. Can you maintain your growth without detracting from the factors that have contributed to your success?
<--- Score

61. Can the crisis be isolated to a specific area?
<--- Score

62. How did all of responders know who was in charge at any given time?
<--- Score

63. How do you maintain Incident and Crisis Management's Integrity?
<--- Score

64. If your customer were your grandmother, would you tell her to buy what you're selling?
<--- Score

65. What are you challenging?
<--- Score

66. What is it like to work for you?
<--- Score

67. Are there search/rescue services available locally?
<--- Score

68. What, if any, search efforts have been initiated?
<--- Score

69. How do you set Incident and Crisis Management stretch targets and how do you get people to not only participate in setting these stretch targets but also that they strive to achieve these?
<--- Score

70. Are you using a design thinking approach and integrating Innovation, Incident and Crisis Management Experience, and Brand Value?
<--- Score

71. Can the schedule be done in the given time?
<--- Score

72. Instead of going to current contacts for new ideas, what if you reconnected with dormant contacts-- the people you used to know? If you were going reactivate a dormant tie, who would it be?
<--- Score

73. What is the kind of project structure that would be appropriate for your Incident and Crisis Management project, should it be formal and complex, or can it be less formal and relatively simple?
<--- Score

74. How do you keep records, of what?
<--- Score

75. If you do not follow, then how to lead?
<--- Score

76. How likely is it that a customer would recommend your company to a friend or colleague?
<--- Score

77. Who is responsible for errors?
<--- Score

78. What have you done to protect your business from competitive encroachment?
<--- Score

79. What is the overall talent health of your organization as a whole at senior levels, and for each organization reporting to a member of the Senior Leadership Team?
<--- Score

80. How is implementation research currently incorporated into each of your goals?
<--- Score

81. What are your most important goals for the strategic Incident and Crisis Management objectives?
<--- Score

82. What happens if you do not have enough funding?
<--- Score

83. What one word do you want to own in the minds of your customers, employees, and partners?
<--- Score

84. What goals did you miss?
<--- Score

85. Are you paying enough attention to the partners your company depends on to succeed?
<--- Score

86. How do you foster the skills, knowledge, talents, attributes, and characteristics you want to have?
<--- Score

87. Do you have enough freaky customers in your portfolio pushing you to the limit day in and day out?
<--- Score

88. Can you break it down?
<--- Score

89. What knowledge, skills and characteristics mark a good Incident and Crisis Management project manager?
<--- Score

90. Is your basic point _____ or _____?
<--- Score

91. What Incident and Crisis Management modifications can you make work for you?
<--- Score

92. What are known details of incident?
<--- Score

93. Who do you think the world wants your organization to be?
<--- Score

94. Do you have the right people on the bus?
<--- Score

95. If you got fired and a new hire took your place, what would she do different?

<--- Score

96. Why is Incident and Crisis Management important for you now?
<--- Score

97. How do you track customer value, profitability or financial return, organizational success, and sustainability?
<--- Score

98. Who have you, as a company, historically been when you've been at your best?
<--- Score

99. How do you transition from the baseline to the target?
<--- Score

100. What would have to be true for the option on the table to be the best possible choice?
<--- Score

101. What are you trying to prove to yourself, and how might it be hijacking your life and business success?
<--- Score

102. When information truly is ubiquitous, when reach and connectivity are completely global, when computing resources are infinite, and when a whole new set of impossibilities are not only possible, but happening, what will that do to your business?
<--- Score

103. What stupid rule would you most like to kill?
<--- Score

104. Do you structure your organization based on the Incident Command System?
<--- Score

105. What are the top 3 things at the forefront of your Incident and Crisis Management agendas for the next 3 years?
<--- Score

106. Operational - will it work?
<--- Score

107. Is there a work around that you can use?
<--- Score

108. Is it economical; do you have the time and money?
<--- Score

109. Are all key stakeholders present at all Structured Walkthroughs?
<--- Score

110. Do you know what you are doing? And who do you call if you don't?
<--- Score

111. What was your chief source of reliable information during the incident?
<--- Score

112. Whom among your colleagues do you trust, and for what?
<--- Score

113. Is safety of the group an immediate concern?
<--- Score

114. How do you lead with Incident and Crisis Management in mind?
<--- Score

115. Which communication channels would you be able/unable to use, and what is your back up?
<--- Score

116. How can you negotiate Incident and Crisis Management successfully with a stubborn boss, an irate client, or a deceitful coworker?
<--- Score

117. How will you go about returning to full operations?
<--- Score

118. Who is responsible for Incident and Crisis Management?
<--- Score

119. Who, on the executive team or the board, has spoken to a customer recently?
<--- Score

120. Is the emergency coordination team or the crisis management team in charge?
<--- Score

121. What are the rules and assumptions your industry operates under? What if the opposite were true?
<--- Score

122. Whose voice (department, ethnic group, women, older workers, etc) might you have missed hearing from in your company, and how might you amplify this voice to create positive momentum for your business?
<--- Score

123. What are your personal philosophies regarding Incident and Crisis Management and how do they influence your work?
<--- Score

124. At what moment would you think; Will I get fired?
<--- Score

125. What are the key enablers to make this Incident and Crisis Management move?
<--- Score

126. What is your competitive advantage?
<--- Score

127. Are the criteria for selecting recommendations stated?
<--- Score

128. Do you have an implicit bias for capital investments over people investments?
<--- Score

129. Do Incident and Crisis Management rules make a reasonable demand on a users capabilities?
<--- Score

130. Are you satisfied with your current role? If not, what is missing from it?

<--- Score

131. What are the success criteria that will indicate that Incident and Crisis Management objectives have been met and the benefits delivered?
<--- Score

132. Did you receive enough information and timely updates?
<--- Score

133. What was the last experiment you ran?
<--- Score

134. What could happen if you do not do it?
<--- Score

135. Which individuals, teams or departments will be involved in Incident and Crisis Management?
<--- Score

136. What are the potential basics of Incident and Crisis Management fraud?
<--- Score

137. Why will customers want to buy your organizations products/services?
<--- Score

138. Is Incident and Crisis Management dependent on the successful delivery of a current project?
<--- Score

139. Think of your Incident and Crisis Management project, what are the main functions?
<--- Score

140. What is something you believe that nearly no one agrees with you on?
<--- Score

141. Who is the local emergency manager?
<--- Score

142. What are the usability implications of Incident and Crisis Management actions?
<--- Score

143. Which models, tools and techniques are necessary?
<--- Score

144. In the past year, what have you done (or could you have done) to increase the accurate perception of your company/brand as ethical and honest?
<--- Score

145. How do you keep the momentum going?
<--- Score

146. How important is Incident and Crisis Management to the user organizations mission?
<--- Score

147. Do you have an emergency or a crisis?
<--- Score

148. Are you changing as fast as the world around you?
<--- Score

149. Is a Incident and Crisis Management

breakthrough on the horizon?
<--- Score

150. Are your responses positive or negative?
<--- Score

151. What do we do when new problems arise?
<--- Score

152. What relationships among Incident and Crisis Management trends do you perceive?
<--- Score

153. Have you been approached by the media?
<--- Score

154. What are specific Incident and Crisis Management rules to follow?
<--- Score

155. How will you motivate the stakeholders with the least vested interest?
<--- Score

156. If your company went out of business tomorrow, would anyone who doesn't get a paycheck here care?
<--- Score

157. What is the estimated value of the project?
<--- Score

158. What you are going to do to affect the numbers?
<--- Score

159. What trophy do you want on your mantle?
<--- Score

160. What percentage of people/products is likely to be affected?

<--- Score

161. What is the source of the strategies for Incident and Crisis Management strengthening and reform?

<--- Score

162. What may be the consequences for the performance of an organization if all stakeholders are not consulted regarding Incident and Crisis Management?

<--- Score

163. Are you making progress, and are you making progress as Incident and Crisis Management leaders?

<--- Score

164. Is the Incident and Crisis Management organization completing tasks effectively and efficiently?

<--- Score

165. Does anyone know or have an idea about where the person went?

<--- Score

166. What message must you convey to each stakeholder?

<--- Score

167. What are the best communication channels?

<--- Score

168. What are current Incident and Crisis Management

paradigms?
<--- Score

169. What information is critical to your organization that your executives are ignoring?
<--- Score

170. How do you stay inspired?
<--- Score

171. Who will manage the integration of tools?
<--- Score

172. Do you say no to customers for no reason?
<--- Score

173. How do you ensure that implementations of Incident and Crisis Management products are done in a way that ensures safety?
<--- Score

174. What would you recommend your friend do if he/she were facing this dilemma?
<--- Score

175. What is the overall business strategy?
<--- Score

176. Have new benefits been realized?
<--- Score

177. What will be the consequences to the stakeholder (financial, reputation etc) if Incident and Crisis Management does not go ahead or fails to deliver the objectives?
<--- Score

178. What Incident and Crisis Management skills are most important?
<--- Score

179. What is the nature of the unrest / disaster?
<--- Score

180. What are the short and long-term Incident and Crisis Management goals?
<--- Score

181. Do you have past Incident and Crisis Management successes?
<--- Score

182. What types of duties would you be likely to perform?
<--- Score

183. Do you know who is a friend or a foe?
<--- Score

184. To whom do you add value?
<--- Score

185. How do you govern and fulfill your societal responsibilities?
<--- Score

186. What products have been affected?
<--- Score

187. When will the product be back on sale?
<--- Score

188. How do you know if you are successful?
<--- Score

189. Is the impact that Incident and Crisis Management has shown?
<--- Score

190. What happens at your organization when people fail?
<--- Score

191. Why do and why don't your customers like your organization?
<--- Score

192. Who was involved in the incident?
<--- Score

193. What have been your experiences in defining long range Incident and Crisis Management goals?
<--- Score

194. When and where was the missing person last seen?
<--- Score

195. What source did communications personnel consult for correct technical protocols and procedures?
<--- Score

196. In retrospect, of the projects that you pulled the plug on, what percent do you wish had been allowed to keep going, and what percent do you wish had ended earlier?
<--- Score

197. What potential megatrends could make your business model obsolete?
<--- Score

198. Where would your organization deploy?
<--- Score

199. What are the gaps in your knowledge and experience?
<--- Score

200. How much contingency will be available in the budget?
<--- Score

201. Has implementation been effective in reaching specified objectives so far?
<--- Score

202. How do you determine the key elements that affect Incident and Crisis Management workforce satisfaction, how are these elements determined for different workforce groups and segments?
<--- Score

203. In a project to restructure Incident and Crisis Management outcomes, which stakeholders would you involve?
<--- Score

204. How long will it take to change?
<--- Score

205. How will you know that the Incident and Crisis Management project has been successful?

<--- Score

206. How do senior leaders deploy your organizations vision and values through your leadership system, to the workforce, to key suppliers and partners, and to customers and other stakeholders, as appropriate?
<--- Score

207. How do you accomplish your long range Incident and Crisis Management goals?
<--- Score

208. What is your Incident and Crisis Management strategy?
<--- Score

209. Do you think you know, or do you know you know ?
<--- Score

210. What is your BATNA (best alternative to a negotiated agreement)?
<--- Score

211. How do customers see your organization?
<--- Score

212. How much does Incident and Crisis Management help?
<--- Score

213. What management system can you use to leverage the Incident and Crisis Management experience, ideas, and concerns of the people closest to the work to be done?
<--- Score

214. What is effective Incident and Crisis Management?
<--- Score

215. What business benefits will Incident and Crisis Management goals deliver if achieved?
<--- Score

216. Who is responsible for ensuring appropriate resources (time, people and money) are allocated to Incident and Crisis Management?
<--- Score

217. What are the business goals Incident and Crisis Management is aiming to achieve?
<--- Score

218. How is the crisis being reported in the media?
<--- Score

219. How do you go about securing Incident and Crisis Management?
<--- Score

220. Are you / should you be revolutionary or evolutionary?
<--- Score

221. What does your signature ensure?
<--- Score

222. Were lessons learned captured and communicated?
<--- Score

223. How do you create buy-in?
<--- Score

224. What role does communication play in the success or failure of a Incident and Crisis Management project?
<--- Score

225. If you had to rebuild your organization without any traditional competitive advantages (i.e., no killer technology, promising research, innovative product/service delivery model, etcetera), how would your people have to approach their work and collaborate together in order to create the necessary conditions for success?
<--- Score

226. Is maximizing Incident and Crisis Management protection the same as minimizing Incident and Crisis Management loss?
<--- Score

227. Who will be responsible for deciding whether Incident and Crisis Management goes ahead or not after the initial investigations?
<--- Score

228. Why should people listen to you?
<--- Score

229. Who do you want your customers to become?
<--- Score

230. What are the long-term Incident and Crisis Management goals?
<--- Score

231. Who are your customers?
<--- Score

232. How can you become the company that would put you out of business?
<--- Score

233. Is Incident and Crisis Management realistic, or are you setting yourself up for failure?
<--- Score

234. Which Incident and Crisis Management goals are the most important?
<--- Score

235. What should you stop doing?
<--- Score

236. Where can you break convention?
<--- Score

237. Who is the main stakeholder, with ultimate responsibility for driving Incident and Crisis Management forward?
<--- Score

238. Are you maintaining a past–present–future perspective throughout the Incident and Crisis Management discussion?
<--- Score

239. Who are the key stakeholders?
<--- Score

Add up total points for this section:

_____ = Total points for this section

Divided by: _____ (number of statements answered) = _____
Average score for this section

Transfer your score to the Incident and Crisis Management Index at the beginning of the Self-Assessment.

Incident and Crisis Management and Managing Projects, Criteria for Project Managers:

1.0 Initiating Process Group: Incident and Crisis Management

1. What technical work to do in each phase?

2. What is the NEXT thing to do?

3. What communication items need improvement?

4. Did the Incident and Crisis Management project team have the right skills?

5. The Incident and Crisis Management project managers have maximum authority in which type of organization?

6. Did you use a contractor or vendor?

7. What is the stake of others in your Incident and Crisis Management project?

8. The Incident and Crisis Management project you are managing has nine stakeholders. How many channel of communications are there between corresponding stakeholders?

9. Do you understand the quality and control criteria that must be achieved for successful Incident and Crisis Management project completion?

10. Information sharing?

11. Based on your Incident and Crisis Management project communication management plan, what worked well?

12. Do you understand the communication expectations for this Incident and Crisis Management project?

13. Do you know if the Incident and Crisis Management project requires outside equipment or vendor resources?

14. Are there resources to maintain and support the outcome of the Incident and Crisis Management project?

15. What areas were overlooked on this Incident and Crisis Management project?

16. Were resources available as planned?

17. Do you know the Incident and Crisis Management projects goal, purpose and objectives?

18. How do you help others satisfy needs?

19. What will be the pressing issues of tomorrow?

20. How will you do it?

1.1 Project Charter: Incident and Crisis Management

21. Why do you manage integration?

22. What outcome, in measureable terms, are you hoping to accomplish?

23. Avoid costs, improve service, and/ or comply with a mandate?

24. Market – identify products market, including whether it is outside of the objective: what is the purpose of the program or Incident and Crisis Management project?

25. What does it need to do?

26. What are you striving to accomplish (measurable goal(s))?

27. Customer benefits: what customer requirements does this Incident and Crisis Management project address?

28. How will you learn more about the process or system you are trying to improve?

29. Are you building in-house ?

30. What is the justification?

31. Why use a Incident and Crisis Management project

charter?

32. When?

33. How high should you set your goals?

34. Run it as as a startup?

35. How will you know that a change is an improvement?

36. What is the business need?

37. For whom?

38. What material?

39. Customer: who are you doing the Incident and Crisis Management project for?

40. Pop quiz – which are the same inputs as in the Incident and Crisis Management project charter?

1.2 Stakeholder Register: Incident and Crisis Management

41. Who wants to talk about Security?

42. How will reports be created?

43. What & Why?

44. Is your organization ready for change?

45. How should employers make voices heard?

46. What is the power of the stakeholder?

47. Who is managing stakeholder engagement?

48. How big is the gap?

49. How much influence do they have on the Incident and Crisis Management project?

50. What opportunities exist to provide communications?

51. Who are the stakeholders?

52. What are the major Incident and Crisis Management project milestones requiring communications or providing communications opportunities?

1.3 Stakeholder Analysis Matrix: Incident and Crisis Management

53. How do you manage Incident and Crisis Management project Risk?

54. Who has not been involved up to now and should have been?

55. Participatory approach: how will key stakeholders participate in the Incident and Crisis Management project?

56. What resources might the stakeholder bring to the Incident and Crisis Management project?

57. Who has the power to influence the outcomes of the work?

58. Who has control over whom?

59. Do any safeguard policies apply to the Incident and Crisis Management project?

60. Reliability of data, plan predictability?

61. How to measure the achievement of the Outputs?

62. Who is influential in the Incident and Crisis Management project area (both thematic and geographic areas)?

63. How are you predicting what future (work)loads

will be?

64. Reputation, presence and reach?

65. Who will be affected by the Incident and Crisis Management project?

66. What tools would help you communicate?

67. Could any of your organizations weaknesses seriously threaten development?

68. Vital contracts and partners?

69. What are the mechanisms of public and social accountability, and how can they be made better?

70. Philosophy and values?

71. Is changing technology threatening your organizations position?

72. What can the Incident and Crisis Management projects outcome be used for?

2.0 Planning Process Group: Incident and Crisis Management

73. Do the partners have sufficient financial capacity to keep up the benefits produced by the programme?

74. To what extent has a PMO contributed to raising the quality of the design of the Incident and Crisis Management project?

75. Did the program design/ implementation strategy adequately address the planning stage necessary to set up structures, hire staff etc.?

76. How well will the chosen processes produce the expected results?

77. What makes your Incident and Crisis Management project successful?

78. How well do the team follow the chosen processes?

79. You are creating your WBS and find that you keep decomposing tasks into smaller and smaller units. How can you tell when you are done?

80. Explanation: is what the Incident and Crisis Management project intents to solve a hard question?

81. What are the different approaches to building the WBS?

82. Mitigate. what will you do to minimize the impact should a risk event occur?

83. To what extent and in what ways are the Incident and Crisis Management project contributing to progress towards organizational reform?

84. To what extent do the intervention objectives and strategies of the Incident and Crisis Management project respond to your organizations plans?

85. How well did the chosen processes fit the needs of the Incident and Crisis Management project?

86. How should needs be met?

87. In what ways can the governance of the Incident and Crisis Management project be improved so that it has greater likelihood of achieving future sustainability?

88. What is involved in Incident and Crisis Management project scope management, and why is good Incident and Crisis Management project scope management so important on information technology Incident and Crisis Management projects?

89. Does it make any difference if you are successful?

90. What is the critical path for this Incident and Crisis Management project, and what is the duration of the critical path?

91. To what extent has the intervention strategy been adapted to the areas of intervention in which it is being implemented?

92. Does the program have follow-up mechanisms (to verify the quality of the products, punctuality of delivery, etc.) to measure progress in the achievement of the envisaged results?

2.1 Project Management Plan: Incident and Crisis Management

93. Is the appropriate plan selected based on your organizations objectives and evaluation criteria expressed in Principles and Guidelines policies?

94. When is a Incident and Crisis Management project management plan created?

95. What are the known stakeholder requirements?

96. Is mitigation authorized or recommended?

97. What data/reports/tools/etc. do program managers need?

98. Are the existing and future without-plan conditions reasonable and appropriate?

99. What should you drop in order to add something new?

100. What are the training needs?

101. What are the assigned resources?

102. Is the budget realistic?

103. Who is the Incident and Crisis Management project Manager?

104. How do you organize the costs in the Incident

and Crisis Management project management plan?

105. What happened during the process that you found interesting?

106. Are the proposed Incident and Crisis Management project purposes different than a previously authorized Incident and Crisis Management project?

107. Is the engineering content at a feasibility level-of-detail, and is it sufficiently complete, to provide an adequate basis for the baseline cost estimate?

108. Does the selected plan protect privacy?

109. What is risk management?

110. What are the deliverables?

111. Who manages integration?

2.2 Scope Management Plan: Incident and Crisis Management

112. What do you need to do to accomplish the goal or goals?

113. Describe how the deliverables will be verified against the Incident and Crisis Management project scope. To whom will the deliverables be first presented for inspection and verification?

114. Process groups – where do scope management processes fit in?

115. Has a capability assessment been conducted?

116. Are staff skills known and available for each task?

117. Given the scope of the Incident and Crisis Management project, which criterion should be optimized?

118. Did your Incident and Crisis Management project ask for this?

119. Timeline and milestones?

120. Are calculations and results of analyzes essentially correct?

121. Does the Incident and Crisis Management project have a Statement of Work?

122. What is your organizations history in doing similar activities?

123. During what part of the PM process is the Incident and Crisis Management project scope statement created?

124. Are Incident and Crisis Management project contact logs kept up to date?

125. Are there any windfall benefits that would accrue to the Incident and Crisis Management project sponsor or other parties?

126. Pop quiz – which are the same inputs as in scope planning?

127. What weaknesses do you have?

128. Have the key elements of a coherent Incident and Crisis Management project management strategy been established?

129. What is the need the Incident and Crisis Management project will address?

130. Are decisions captured in a decisions log?

131. What does the critical path really mean?

2.3 Requirements Management Plan: Incident and Crisis Management

132. Will you have access to stakeholders when you need them?

133. To see if a requirement statement is sufficiently well-defined, read it from the developers perspective. Mentally add the phrase, call me when youre done to the end of the requirement and see if that makes you nervous. In other words, would you need additional clarification from the author to understand the requirement well enough to design and implement it?

134. Have stakeholders been instructed in the Change Control process?

135. What went wrong?

136. Do you have an appropriate arrangement for meetings?

137. How will the information be distributed?

138. Do you really need to write this document at all?

139. Subject to change control?

140. Will you use tracing to help understand the impact of a change in requirements?

141. Who came up with this requirement?

142. What information regarding the Incident and Crisis Management project requirements will be reported?

143. Why manage requirements?

144. Is stakeholder risk tolerance an important factor for the requirements process in this Incident and Crisis Management project?

145. How detailed should the Incident and Crisis Management project get?

146. What are you trying to do?

147. Did you use declarative statements?

148. How will bidders price evaluations be done, by deliverables, phases, or in a big bang?

149. Who will initially review the Incident and Crisis Management project work or products to ensure it meets the applicable acceptance criteria?

150. Will the Incident and Crisis Management project requirements become approved in writing?

151. Is the system software (non-operating system) new to the IT Incident and Crisis Management project team?

2.4 Requirements Documentation: Incident and Crisis Management

152. Is the requirement realistically testable?

153. Can the requirements be checked?

154. How much does requirements engineering cost?

155. What images does it conjure?

156. Verifiability. can the requirements be checked?

157. Where are business rules being captured?

158. How do you get the user to tell you what they want?

159. What is effective documentation?

160. What are the attributes of a customer?

161. What is a show stopper in the requirements?

162. Can you check system requirements?

163. Validity. does the system provide the functions which best support the customers needs?

164. What can tools do for us?

165. How will requirements be documented and who signs off on them?

166. How does what is being described meet the business need?

167. Have the benefits identified with the system being identified clearly?

168. Do your constraints stand?

169. How to document system requirements?

170. Does your organization restrict technical alternatives?

171. Does the system provide the functions which best support the customers needs?

2.5 Requirements Traceability Matrix: Incident and Crisis Management

172. Will you use a Requirements Traceability Matrix?

173. Describe the process for approving requirements so they can be added to the traceability matrix and Incident and Crisis Management project work can be performed. Will the Incident and Crisis Management project requirements become approved in writing?

174. How will it affect the stakeholders personally in career?

175. Why do you manage scope?

176. Why use a WBS?

177. How do you manage scope?

178. What percentage of Incident and Crisis Management projects are producing traceability matrices between requirements and other work products?

179. How small is small enough?

180. What are the chronologies, contingencies, consequences, criteria?

181. What is the WBS?

182. Is there a requirements traceability process in

place?

183. Do you have a clear understanding of all subcontracts in place?

2.6 Project Scope Statement: Incident and Crisis Management

184. Have the configuration management functions been assigned?

185. Identify how your team and you will create the Incident and Crisis Management project scope statement and the work breakdown structure (WBS). Document how you will create the Incident and Crisis Management project scope statement and WBS, and make sure you answer the following questions: In defining Incident and Crisis Management project scope and the WBS, will you and your Incident and Crisis Management project team be using methods defined by your organization, methods defined by the Incident and Crisis Management project management office (PMO), or other methods?

186. Are there adequate Incident and Crisis Management project control systems?

187. Once its defined, what is the stability of the Incident and Crisis Management project scope?

188. Write a brief purpose statement for this Incident and Crisis Management project. Include a business justification statement. What is the product of this Incident and Crisis Management project?

189. Will all Incident and Crisis Management project issues be unconditionally tracked through the issue resolution process?

190. What is the product of this Incident and Crisis Management project?

191. Incident and Crisis Management project lead, team lead, solution architect?

192. Is the plan for your organization of the Incident and Crisis Management project resources adequate?

193. Do you anticipate new stakeholders joining the Incident and Crisis Management project over time?

194. Is the plan under configuration management?

195. Is the change control process documented and on file?

196. Is this process communicated to the customer and team members?

197. Change management vs. change leadership - what is the difference?

198. If there is an independent oversight contractor, have they signed off on the Incident and Crisis Management project Plan?

199. Any new risks introduced or old risks impacted. Are there issues that could affect the existing requirements for the result, service, or product if the scope changes?

200. Were potential customers involved early in the planning process?

201. Where and how does the team fit within your organization structure?

202. What process would you recommend for creating the Incident and Crisis Management project scope statement?

2.7 Assumption and Constraint Log: Incident and Crisis Management

203. Has a Incident and Crisis Management project Communications Plan been developed?

204. Are funding and staffing resource estimates sufficiently detailed and documented for use in planning and tracking the Incident and Crisis Management project?

205. What threats might prevent you from getting there?

206. Are there nonconformance issues?

207. Is this process still needed?

208. Were the system requirements formally reviewed prior to initiating the design phase?

209. What would you gain if you spent time working to improve this process?

210. Are you meeting your customers expectations consistently?

211. Is there a Steering Committee in place?

212. How can constraints be violated?

213. How many Incident and Crisis Management project staff does this specific process affect?

214. Are there ways to reduce the time it takes to get something approved?

215. Are there processes in place to ensure that all the terms and code concepts have been documented consistently?

216. Does a specific action and/or state that is known to violate security policy occur?

217. Would known impacts serve as impediments?

218. Violation trace: why ?

219. Is the current scope of the Incident and Crisis Management project substantially different than that originally defined in the approved Incident and Crisis Management project plan?

220. Have all necessary approvals been obtained?

2.8 Work Breakdown Structure: Incident and Crisis Management

221. Is it still viable?

222. Why is it useful?

223. Can you make it?

224. Who has to do it?

225. Where does it take place?

226. When does it have to be done?

227. What has to be done?

228. How big is a work-package?

229. What is the probability of completing the Incident and Crisis Management project in less that xx days?

230. Why would you develop a Work Breakdown Structure?

231. When do you stop?

232. Is the work breakdown structure (wbs) defined and is the scope of the Incident and Crisis Management project clear with assigned deliverable owners?

233. What is the probability that the Incident and Crisis Management project duration will exceed xx weeks?

234. When would you develop a Work Breakdown Structure?

235. How will you and your Incident and Crisis Management project team define the Incident and Crisis Management projects scope and work breakdown structure?

236. How far down?

2.9 WBS Dictionary: Incident and Crisis Management

237. Are procedures in existence that control replanning of unopened work packages, and are corresponding procedures adhered to?

238. Are overhead costs budgets established on a basis consistent with anticipated direct business base?

239. Is subcontracted work defined and identified to the appropriate subcontractor within the proper WBS element?

240. Are records maintained to show full accountability for all material purchased for the contract, including the residual inventory?

241. Identify potential or actual budget-based and time-based schedule variances?

242. Are current budgets resulting from changes to the authorized work and/or internal replanning, reconcilable to original budgets for specified reporting items?

243. Do work packages consist of discrete tasks which are adequately described?

244. Does the contractors system identify work accomplishment against the schedule plan?

245. Are detailed work packages planned as far in advance as practicable?

246. Evaluate the performance of operating organizations?

247. Does the scheduling system identify in a timely manner the status of work?

248. Are retroactive changes to budgets for completed work specifically prohibited in an established procedure, and is this procedure adhered to?

249. Does the contractors system provide for the determination of cost variances attributable to the excess usage of material?

250. Is all contract work included in the CWBS?

251. Changes in the direct base to which overhead costs are allocated?

252. Do work packages reflect the actual way in which the work will be done and are they meaningful products or management-oriented subdivisions of a higher level element of work?

253. Actual cost of work performed?

254. Are the latest revised estimates of costs at completion compared with the established budgets at appropriate levels and causes of variances identified?

255. Software specification, development, integration,

and testing, licenses ?

2.10 Schedule Management Plan: Incident and Crisis Management

256. Has a structured approach been used to break work effort into manageable components (WBS)?

257. Are the Incident and Crisis Management project team members located locally to the users/ stakeholders?

258. Has the scope management document been updated and distributed to help prevent scope creep?

259. Is the quality assurance team identified?

260. Is there an excessive and invalid use of task constraints and relationships of leads/lags?

261. Is quality monitored from the perspective of the customers needs and expectations?

262. Is the assigned Incident and Crisis Management project manager a PMP (Certified Incident and Crisis Management project manager) and experienced?

263. Do Incident and Crisis Management project teams & team members report on status / activities / progress?

264. Are all activities captured and do they address all approved work scope in the Incident and Crisis Management project baseline?

265. Are vendor invoices audited for accuracy before payment?

266. Are cause and effect determined for risks when they occur?

267. How are Incident and Crisis Management projects different from operations?

268. Is there anything planned that does not need to be here?

269. Are enough systems & user personnel assigned to the Incident and Crisis Management project?

270. Is there a procedure for management, control and release of schedule margin?

271. Are tasks tracked by hours?

272. Has your organization readiness assessment been conducted?

273. Are the payment terms being followed?

274. What is the difference between % Complete and % work?

2.11 Activity List: Incident and Crisis Management

275. When do the individual activities need to start and finish?

276. How much slack is available in the Incident and Crisis Management project?

277. In what sequence?

278. Can you determine the activity that must finish, before this activity can start?

279. How do you determine the late start (LS) for each activity?

280. What will be performed?

281. Who will perform the work?

282. How detailed should a Incident and Crisis Management project get?

283. How can the Incident and Crisis Management project be displayed graphically to better visualize the activities?

284. For other activities, how much delay can be tolerated?

285. How difficult will it be to do specific activities on this Incident and Crisis Management project?

286. How should ongoing costs be monitored to try to keep the Incident and Crisis Management project within budget?

287. What is the total time required to complete the Incident and Crisis Management project if no delays occur?

288. What is the LF and LS for each activity?

289. What are the critical bottleneck activities?

290. How will it be performed?

291. What did not go as well?

2.12 Activity Attributes: Incident and Crisis Management

292. Can you re-assign any activities to another resource to resolve an over-allocation?

293. Time for overtime?

294. How many days do you need to complete the work scope with a limit of X number of resources?

295. Were there other ways you could have organized the data to achieve similar results?

296. Do you feel very comfortable with your prediction?

297. What is the general pattern here?

298. Have you identified the Activity Leveling Priority code value on each activity?

299. Resources to accomplish the work?

300. How do you manage time?

301. What activity do you think you should spend the most time on?

302. Resource is assigned to?

303. Is there a trend during the year?

304. What is missing?

305. Activity: fair or not fair?

306. How much activity detail is required?

307. What conclusions/generalizations can you draw from this?

308. Where else does it apply?

309. Does your organization of the data change its meaning?

2.13 Milestone List: Incident and Crisis Management

310. Usps (unique selling points)?

311. How late can the activity start?

312. It is to be a narrative text providing the crucial aspects of your Incident and Crisis Management project proposal answering what, who, how, when and where?

313. Insurmountable weaknesses?

314. How will you get the word out to customers?

315. When will the Incident and Crisis Management project be complete?

316. Which path is the critical path?

317. New USPs?

318. Sustaining internal capabilities?

319. How soon can the activity start?

320. How will the milestone be verified?

321. Continuity, supply chain robustness?

322. Do you foresee any technical risks or developmental challenges?

323. Obstacles faced?

324. Can you derive how soon can the whole Incident and Crisis Management project finish?

325. Loss of key staff?

326. Gaps in capabilities?

327. Legislative effects?

328. What specific improvements did you make to the Incident and Crisis Management project proposal since the previous time?

2.14 Network Diagram: Incident and Crisis Management

329. Are the required resources available?

330. What activities must follow this activity?

331. What job or jobs precede it?

332. What activity must be completed immediately before this activity can start?

333. What are the Key Success Factors?

334. What are the Major Administrative Issues?

335. What must be completed before an activity can be started?

336. Will crashing x weeks return more in benefits than it costs?

337. How difficult will it be to do specific activities on this Incident and Crisis Management project?

338. What is the probability of completing the Incident and Crisis Management project in less that xx days?

339. If the Incident and Crisis Management project network diagram cannot change and you have extra personnel resources, what is the BEST thing to do?

340. Which type of network diagram allows you to depict four types of dependencies?

341. Exercise: what is the probability that the Incident and Crisis Management project duration will exceed xx weeks?

342. Where do you schedule uncertainty time?

343. What controls the start and finish of a job?

344. How confident can you be in your milestone dates and the delivery date?

345. Why must you schedule milestones, such as reviews, throughout the Incident and Crisis Management project?

346. Are the gantt chart and/or network diagram updated periodically and used to assess the overall Incident and Crisis Management project timetable?

347. What are the tools?

2.15 Activity Resource Requirements: Incident and Crisis Management

348. What is the Work Plan Standard?

349. When does monitoring begin?

350. Other support in specific areas?

351. Why do you do that?

352. How many signatures do you require on a check and does this match what is in your policy and procedures?

353. Anything else?

354. How do you handle petty cash?

355. Which logical relationship does the PDM use most often?

356. Do you use tools like decomposition and rolling-wave planning to produce the activity list and other outputs?

357. What are constraints that you might find during the Human Resource Planning process?

358. Are there unresolved issues that need to be addressed?

359. Organizational Applicability?

2.16 Resource Breakdown Structure: Incident and Crisis Management

360. What defines a successful Incident and Crisis Management project?

361. What can you do to improve productivity?

362. Which resources should be in the resource pool?

363. Who delivers the information?

364. Any changes from stakeholders?

365. Changes based on input from stakeholders?

366. How can this help you with team building?

367. The list could probably go on, but, the thing that you would most like to know is, How long & How much?

368. Who will be used as a Incident and Crisis Management project team member?

369. Goals for the Incident and Crisis Management project. What is each stakeholders desired outcome for the Incident and Crisis Management project?

370. What went right?

371. Why time management?

372. Who is allowed to see what data about which resources?

373. How difficult will it be to do specific activities on this Incident and Crisis Management project?

2.17 Activity Duration Estimates: Incident and Crisis Management

374. Is corrective action taken to bring Incident and Crisis Management project performance into line with the Incident and Crisis Management project plan?

375. Are the causes of all variances identified?

376. Do you think many other organizations could apply this methodology, or does each organization need to create its own methodology?

377. Why should Incident and Crisis Management project managers strive to make jobs look easy?

378. What are the Incident and Crisis Management project management deliverables of each process group?

379. Is evaluation criteria defined to rate proposals?

380. Why do you think schedule issues often cause the most conflicts on Incident and Crisis Management projects?

381. Why is activity definition the first process involved in Incident and Crisis Management project time management?

382. What type of contract was used and why?

383. Do stakeholders follow a procedure for formally

accepting the Incident and Crisis Management project scope?

384. Consider the changes in the job market for information technology workers. How does the job market and current state of the economy affect human resource management?

385. Is earned value analysis completed to assess Incident and Crisis Management project performance?

386. Which best describes the relationship between standard deviation and risk?

387. Write a oneto two-page paper describing your dream team for this Incident and Crisis Management project. What type of people would you want on your team?

388. Are inspections completed to determine if the results comply with the requirements?

389. Which includes asking team members about the time estimates for activities and reaching agreement on the calendar date for each activity?

390. What is done after activity duration estimation?

391. Are resource rates available to calculate Incident and Crisis Management project costs?

392. How does a Incident and Crisis Management project life cycle differ from a product life cycle?

393. Is training acquired to enhance the skills,

knowledge and capabilities of the Incident and Crisis Management project team?

2.18 Duration Estimating Worksheet: Incident and Crisis Management

394. What is an Average Incident and Crisis Management project?

395. What info is needed?

396. What utility impacts are there?

397. Is a construction detail attached (to aid in explanation)?

398. Define the work as completely as possible. What work will be included in the Incident and Crisis Management project?

399. Is the Incident and Crisis Management project responsive to community need?

400. When does your organization expect to be able to complete it?

401. Can the Incident and Crisis Management project be constructed as planned?

402. What is next?

403. Does the Incident and Crisis Management project provide innovative ways for stakeholders to overcome obstacles or deliver better outcomes?

404. How can the Incident and Crisis Management

project be displayed graphically to better visualize the activities?

405. Do any colleagues have experience with your organization and/or RFPs?

406. Why estimate costs?

407. Science = process: remember the scientific method?

408. What questions do you have?

409. Will the Incident and Crisis Management project collaborate with the local community and leverage resources?

410. What is the total time required to complete the Incident and Crisis Management project if no delays occur?

2.19 Project Schedule: Incident and Crisis Management

411. Did the Incident and Crisis Management project come in under budget?

412. Master Incident and Crisis Management project schedule?

413. How can you shorten the schedule?

414. Why is software Incident and Crisis Management project disaster so common?

415. What are you counting on?

416. How do you manage Incident and Crisis Management project Risk?

417. Your Incident and Crisis Management project management plan results in a Incident and Crisis Management project schedule that is too long. If the Incident and Crisis Management project network diagram cannot change and you have extra personnel resources, what is the BEST thing to do?

418. Meet requirements?

419. Should you include sub-activities?

420. Is infrastructure setup part of your Incident and Crisis Management project?

421. How do you know that youhave done this right?

422. Activity charts and bar charts are graphical representations of a Incident and Crisis Management project schedule ...how do they differ?

423. It allows the Incident and Crisis Management project to be delivered on schedule. How Do you Use Schedules?

424. Why is this particularly bad?

425. How can you minimize or control changes to Incident and Crisis Management project schedules?

426. Are the original Incident and Crisis Management project schedule and budget realistic?

427. Are procedures defined by which the Incident and Crisis Management project schedule may be changed?

428. Did the final product meet or exceed user expectations?

429. Is the Incident and Crisis Management project schedule available for all Incident and Crisis Management project team members to review?

430. Your best shot for providing estimations how complex/how much work does the activity require?

2.20 Cost Management Plan: Incident and Crisis Management

431. Risk rating?

432. Is current scope of the Incident and Crisis Management project substantially different than that originally defined?

433. What strengths do you have?

434. Why do you manage cost?

435. Were Incident and Crisis Management project team members involved in detailed estimating and scheduling?

436. Best practices implementation – How will change management be applied to this Incident and Crisis Management project?

437. Staffing Requirements?

438. Does the Incident and Crisis Management project have a Quality Culture?

439. Has the budget been baselined?

440. Are changes in scope (deliverable commitments) agreed to by all affected groups & individuals?

441. Are parking lot items captured?

442. Have Incident and Crisis Management project management standards and procedures been identified / established and documented?

443. Is an industry recognized mechanized support tool(s) being used for Incident and Crisis Management project scheduling & tracking?

444. Are changes in deliverable commitments agreed to by all affected groups & individuals?

445. Are all key components of a Quality Assurance Plan present?

446. Is there a set of procedures defining the scope, procedures, and deliverables defining quality control?

447. Are trade-offs between accepting the risk and mitigating the risk identified?

448. What is Incident and Crisis Management project management?

449. Has a resource management plan been created?

2.21 Activity Cost Estimates: Incident and Crisis Management

450. How do you fund change orders?

451. What are you looking for?

452. Was it performed on time?

453. In which phase of the acquisition process cycle does source qualifications reside?

454. What is the Incident and Crisis Management projects sustainability strategy that will ensure Incident and Crisis Management project results will endure or be sustained?

455. Specific - is the objective clear in terms of what, how, when, and where the situation will be changed?

456. Were the costs or charges reasonable?

457. Can you delete activities or make them inactive?

458. What is procurement?

459. Was the consultant knowledgeable about the program?

460. How do you treat administrative costs in the activity inventory?

461. Does the estimator have experience?

462. What areas does the group agree are the biggest success on the Incident and Crisis Management project?

463. Does the activity use a common approach or business function to deliver its results?

464. Who determines when the contractor is paid?

465. How do you manage cost?

466. What were things that you did well, and could improve, and how?

467. How and when do you enter into Incident and Crisis Management project Procurement Management?

468. Who & what determines the need for contracted services?

469. What is your organizations history in doing similar tasks?

2.22 Cost Estimating Worksheet: Incident and Crisis Management

470. Will the Incident and Crisis Management project collaborate with the local community and leverage resources?

471. Is it feasible to establish a control group arrangement?

472. What can be included?

473. What additional Incident and Crisis Management project(s) could be initiated as a result of this Incident and Crisis Management project?

474. Can a trend be established from historical performance data on the selected measure and are the criteria for using trend analysis or forecasting methods met?

475. What costs are to be estimated?

476. What happens to any remaining funds not used?

477. Identify the timeframe necessary to monitor progress and collect data to determine how the selected measure has changed?

478. What will others want?

479. How will the results be shared and to whom?

480. Ask: are others positioned to know, are others credible, and will others cooperate?

481. What is the purpose of estimating?

482. Value pocket identification & quantification what are value pockets?

483. Does the Incident and Crisis Management project provide innovative ways for stakeholders to overcome obstacles or deliver better outcomes?

484. What is the estimated labor cost today based upon this information?

485. Is the Incident and Crisis Management project responsive to community need?

486. Who is best positioned to know and assist in identifying corresponding factors?

2.23 Cost Baseline: Incident and Crisis Management

487. Are you meeting with your team regularly?

488. On budget?

489. When should cost estimates be developed?

490. How difficult will it be to do specific tasks on the Incident and Crisis Management project?

491. Are you asking management for something as a result of this update?

492. Has the Incident and Crisis Management project documentation been archived or otherwise disposed as described in the Incident and Crisis Management project communication plan?

493. Has the Incident and Crisis Management projected annual cost to operate and maintain the product(s) or service(s) been approved and funded?

494. Does it impact schedule, cost, quality?

495. On time?

496. Impact to environment?

497. Have all approved changes to the cost baseline been identified and impact on the Incident and Crisis Management project documented?

498. What is the most important thing to do next to make your Incident and Crisis Management project successful?

499. Verify business objectives. Are others appropriate, and well-articulated?

500. Vac -variance at completion, how much over/under budget do you expect to be?

501. For what purpose ?

502. How likely is it to go wrong?

503. What deliverables come first?

504. Has operations management formally accepted responsibility for operating and maintaining the product(s) or service(s) delivered by the Incident and Crisis Management project?

2.24 Quality Management Plan: Incident and Crisis Management

505. How many Incident and Crisis Management project staff does this specific process affect?

506. How are changes to procedures made?

507. Who gets results of work?

508. How does your organization decide what to measure?

509. How effectively was the Quality Management Plan applied during Incident and Crisis Management project Execution?

510. How does your organization ensure the quality, reliability, and user-friendliness of its hardware and software?

511. How does your organization use comparative data and information to improve organizational performance?

512. How is equipment calibrated?

513. Does the plan conform to standards?

514. Results Available?

515. How do you ensure that protocols are up to date?

516. Do trained quality assurance auditors conduct the audits as defined in the Quality Management Plan and scheduled by the Incident and Crisis Management project manager?

517. Modifications to the requirements?

518. How are senior leaders, employees, and your organization involved in supporting the community?

519. Contradictory information between document sections?

520. Is there a Quality Management Plan?

521. Who else should be involved ?

522. Are requirements management tracking tools and procedures in place?

523. Who do you send data to?

524. How does the material compare to a regulatory threshold?

2.25 Quality Metrics: Incident and Crisis Management

525. Do the operators focus on determining; is there anything you need to worry about?

526. How can the effectiveness of each of the activities be measured?

527. How are requirements conflicts resolved?

528. Is material complete (and does it meet the standards)?

529. How do you measure?

530. What are your organizations next steps?

531. Was the overall quality better or worse than previous products?

532. Subjective quality component: customer satisfaction, how do you measure it?

533. Are there any open risk issues?

534. What does this tell us?

535. What about still open problems?

536. There are many reasons to shore up quality-related metrics, and what metrics are important?

537. What is the benchmark?

538. Has it met internal or external standards?

539. What method of measurement do you use?

540. Are there already quality metrics available that detect nonlinear embeddings and trends similar to the users perception?

541. What is the timeline to meet your goal?

542. Were quality attributes reported?

543. Has risk analysis been adequately reviewed?

544. How do you calculate such metrics?

2.26 Process Improvement Plan: Incident and Crisis Management

545. Where do you want to be?

546. Why do you want to achieve the goal?

547. Does your process ensure quality?

548. What personnel are the champions for the initiative?

549. What is quality and how will you ensure it?

550. Have the frequency of collection and the points in the process where measurements will be made been determined?

551. Where do you focus?

552. Are you making progress on your improvement plan?

553. Purpose of goal: the motive is determined by asking, why do you want to achieve this goal?

554. Everyone agrees on what process improvement is, right?

555. Are you following the quality standards?

556. To elicit goal statements, do you ask a question such as, What do you want to achieve?

557. The motive is determined by asking, Why do you want to achieve this goal?

558. What personnel are the coaches for your initiative?

559. If a process improvement framework is being used, which elements will help the problems and goals listed?

560. Are there forms and procedures to collect and record the data?

561. What personnel are the change agents for your initiative?

562. What makes people good SPI coaches?

2.27 Responsibility Assignment Matrix: Incident and Crisis Management

563. Does the contractor use objective results, design reviews and tests to trace schedule performance?

564. Are management actions taken to reduce indirect costs when there are significant adverse variances?

565. Does the Incident and Crisis Management project need to be analyzed further to uncover additional responsibilities?

566. Is it safe to say you can handle more work or that some tasks you are supposed to do arent worth doing?

567. Cwbs elements to be subcontracted, with identification of subcontractors?

568. How do you assist them to be as productive as possible?

569. Budgets assigned to control accounts?

570. The total budget for the contract (including estimates for authorized and unpriced work)?

571. What tool can show you individual and group allocations?

572. What will the work cost?

573. Budgeted cost for work performed?

574. What is the number one predictor of a groups productivity?

575. Do you need to convince people that its well worth the time and effort?

576. What happens when others get pulled for higher priority Incident and Crisis Management projects?

577. Are meaningful indicators identified for use in measuring the status of cost and schedule performance?

578. Is accountability placed at the lowest-possible level within the Incident and Crisis Management project so that decisions can be made at that level?

579. Too many as: does a proper segregation of duties exist?

580. What do you need to implement earned value management?

2.28 Roles and Responsibilities: Incident and Crisis Management

581. Authority: what areas/Incident and Crisis Management projects in your work do you have the authority to decide upon and act on the already stated decisions?

582. Is there a training program in place for stakeholders covering expectations, roles and responsibilities and any addition knowledge others need to be good stakeholders?

583. What should you highlight for improvement?

584. Who is responsible for implementation activities and where will the functions, roles and responsibilities be defined?

585. Key conclusions and recommendations: Are conclusions and recommendations relevant and acceptable?

586. Have you ever been a part of this team?

587. How is your work-life balance?

588. What should you do now to prepare for your career 5+ years from now?

589. How well did the Incident and Crisis Management project Team understand the expectations of specific roles and responsibilities?

590. Be specific; avoid generalities. Thank you and great work alone are insufficient. What exactly do you appreciate and why?

591. Does your vision/mission support a culture of quality data?

592. What expectations were NOT met?

593. What expectations were met?

594. Are Incident and Crisis Management project team roles and responsibilities identified and documented?

595. Is the data complete?

596. To decide whether to use a quality measurement, ask how will you know when it is achieved?

597. Are your budgets supportive of a culture of quality data?

598. Who: who is involved?

599. What specific behaviors did you observe?

2.29 Human Resource Management Plan: Incident and Crisis Management

600. How are superior performers differentiated from average performers?

601. Is there an approved case?

602. Are estimating assumptions and constraints captured?

603. Is the communication plan being followed?

604. Is the steering committee active in Incident and Crisis Management project oversight?

605. Were Incident and Crisis Management project team members involved in detailed estimating and scheduling?

606. Is it possible to track all classes of Incident and Crisis Management project work (e.g. scheduled, unscheduled, defect repair, etc.)?

607. Have the key elements of a coherent Incident and Crisis Management project management strategy been established?

608. Does the schedule include Incident and Crisis Management project management time and change request analysis time?

609. What skills, knowledge and experiences are

required?

610. Have Incident and Crisis Management project team accountabilities & responsibilities been clearly defined?

611. Quality assurance overheads?

612. Do people have the competencies to meet the strategic objectives?

613. Have stakeholder accountabilities & responsibilities been clearly defined?

614. Did the Incident and Crisis Management project team have the right skills?

615. Has the business need been clearly defined?

616. What is this Incident and Crisis Management project aiming to achieve?

2.30 Communications Management Plan: Incident and Crisis Management

617. Are there common objectives between the team and the stakeholder?

618. Is the stakeholder role recognized by your organization?

619. What is Incident and Crisis Management project communications management?

620. How is this initiative related to other portfolios, programs, or Incident and Crisis Management projects?

621. Why is stakeholder engagement important?

622. What to learn?

623. What is the stakeholders level of authority?

624. In your work, how much time is spent on stakeholder identification?

625. Who to share with?

626. Which team member will work with each stakeholder?

627. How often do you engage with stakeholders?

628. Will messages be directly related to the

release strategy or phases of the Incident and Crisis Management project?

629. Who are the members of the governing body?

630. Who were proponents/opponents?

631. What approaches do you use?

632. Are stakeholders internal or external?

633. What communications method?

634. What help do you and your team need from the stakeholder?

635. Which stakeholders are thought leaders, influences, or early adopters?

2.31 Risk Management Plan: Incident and Crisis Management

636. Financial risk -can your organization afford to undertake the Incident and Crisis Management project?

637. Is there anything you would now do differently on your Incident and Crisis Management project based on this experience?

638. Are enough people available?

639. Do benefits and chances of success outweigh potential damage if success is not attained?

640. Premium on reliability of product?

641. Are there new risks that mitigation strategies might introduce?

642. Who should be notified of the occurrence of each of the indicators?

643. Is the number of people on the Incident and Crisis Management project team adequate to do the job?

644. Management -what contingency plans do you have if the risk becomes a reality?

645. Do you manage the process through use of metrics?

646. Has something like this been done before?

647. What will the damage be?

648. Does the customer understand the software process?

649. Are the participants able to keep up with the workload?

650. Number of users of the product?

651. Havent software Incident and Crisis Management projects been late before?

652. Is the customer willing to commit significant time to the requirements gathering process?

653. Who has experience with this?

654. Risk probability and impact: how will the probabilities and impacts of risk items be assessed?

655. Is the customer willing to participate in reviews?

2.32 Risk Register: Incident and Crisis Management

656. What is a Risk?

657. Contingency actions - planned actions to reduce the immediate seriousness of the risk when it does occur. What should you do when?

658. How well are risks controlled?

659. Who is going to do it?

660. User involvement: do you have the right users?

661. How often will the Risk Management Plan and Risk Register be formally reviewed, and by whom?

662. Financial risk -can your organization afford to undertake the Incident and Crisis Management project?

663. Is further information required before making a decision?

664. How could corresponding Risk affect the Incident and Crisis Management project in terms of cost and schedule?

665. What has changed since the last period?

666. What will be done?

667. Severity Prediction?

668. Budget and schedule: what are the estimated costs and schedules for performing risk-related activities?

669. Technology risk -is the Incident and Crisis Management project technically feasible?

670. What can be done about it?

671. Recovery actions - planned actions taken once a risk has occurred to allow you to move on. What should you do after?

672. How is a Community Risk Register created?

673. Having taken action, how did the responses effect change, and where is the Incident and Crisis Management project now?

674. When will it happen?

2.33 Probability and Impact Assessment: Incident and Crisis Management

675. Does the software engineering team have the right mix of skills?

676. How much is the probability of a risk occurring?

677. How is risk handled within this Incident and Crisis Management project organization?

678. Workarounds are determined during which step of risk management?

679. Risk categorization -which of your categories has more risk than others?

680. What are the preparations required for facing difficulties?

681. How much risk do others need to take?

682. Is the customer willing to establish rapid communication links with the developer?

683. Is the technology to be built new to your organization?

684. What kind of preparation would be required to do this?

685. Are end-users enthusiastically committed to

the Incident and Crisis Management project and the system/product to be built?

686. What risks are necessary to achieve success?

687. Risk data quality assessment - what is the quality of the data used to determine or assess the risk?

688. Do requirements demand the use of new analysis, design, or testing methods?

689. What is the level of experience available with your organization?

690. Prioritized components/features?

691. Are people attending meetings and doing work?

692. What will be the likely political environment during the life of the Incident and Crisis Management project?

693. Are the risk data complete?

2.34 Probability and Impact Matrix: Incident and Crisis Management

694. During which risk management process is a determination to transfer a risk made?

695. What are the chances the risk events will occur?

696. Are the risk data timely and relevant?

697. Is the delay in one subIncident and Crisis Management project going to affect another?

698. Is the present organizational structure for handling the Incident and Crisis Management project sufficient?

699. How to prioritize risks?

700. What is the culture of the market and your organization?

701. Several experts are offsite, and wish to be included. How can this be done?

702. Do you know the order of planning yet?

703. What are the current demands of the customer?

704. Which of your Incident and Crisis Management projects should be selected when compared with other Incident and Crisis Management projects?

705. What can you use the analyzed risks for?

706. What are data sources?

707. Are there alternative opinions/solutions/processes you should explore?

708. What is the likelihood of a breakthrough?

709. How is the risk management process used in practice?

710. How likely is the current plan to come in on schedule or on budget?

711. If you can not fix it, how do you do it differently?

712. Do the people have the right combinations of skills?

2.35 Risk Data Sheet: Incident and Crisis Management

713. Has a sensitivity analysis been carried out?

714. What can you do?

715. Potential for recurrence?

716. What are the main opportunities available to you that you should grab while you can?

717. Will revised controls lead to tolerable risk levels?

718. What do people affected think about the need for, and practicality of preventive measures?

719. What do you know?

720. During work activities could hazards exist?

721. How can hazards be reduced?

722. What are you weak at and therefore need to do better?

723. How reliable is the data source?

724. What are you trying to achieve (Objectives)?

725. Whom do you serve (customers)?

726. Type of risk identified?

727. How do you handle product safely?

728. What can happen?

729. Has the most cost-effective solution been chosen?

730. How can it happen?

2.36 Procurement Management Plan: Incident and Crisis Management

731. Does all Incident and Crisis Management project documentation reside in a common repository for easy access?

732. Is the assigned Incident and Crisis Management project manager a PMP (Certified Incident and Crisis Management project manager) and experienced?

733. Are the Incident and Crisis Management project team members located locally to the users/stakeholders?

734. Were Incident and Crisis Management project team members involved in detailed estimating and scheduling?

735. Was an original risk assessment/risk management plan completed?

736. Were Incident and Crisis Management project team members involved in the development of activity & task decomposition?

737. Is it standard practice to formally commit stakeholders to the Incident and Crisis Management project via agreements?

738. Was the Incident and Crisis Management project schedule reviewed by all stakeholders and formally accepted?

739. Similar Incident and Crisis Management projects?

740. Has the Incident and Crisis Management project manager been identified?

741. What are things that you need to improve?

742. Are risk oriented checklists used during risk identification?

743. Is there a procurement management plan in place?

744. Have all unresolved risks been documented?

745. Are any non-compliance issues that exist communicated to your organization?

2.37 Source Selection Criteria: Incident and Crisis Management

746. What are open book debriefings?

747. What should be considered?

748. How do you encourage efficiency and consistency?

749. In the technical/management area, what criteria do you use to determine the final evaluation ratings?

750. What are the most critical evaluation criteria that prove to be tiebreakers in the evaluation of proposals?

751. When is it appropriate to issue a Draft Request for Proposal (DRFP)?

752. What risks were identified in the proposals?

753. How are clarifications and communications appropriately used?

754. Are there any common areas of weaknesses or deficiencies in the proposals in the competitive range?

755. Is this a cost contract?

756. What evidence should be provided regarding proposal evaluations?

757. What should preproposal conferences accomplish?

758. What is the last item a Incident and Crisis Management project manager must do to finalize Incident and Crisis Management project close-out?

759. Is a cost realism analysis used?

760. How organization are proposed quotes/prices?

761. What does an evaluation address and what does a sample resemble?

762. Who is on the Source Selection Advisory Committee?

763. When is it appropriate to issue a DRFP?

764. Can you make a cost/technical tradeoff?

765. What is price analysis and when should it be performed?

2.38 Stakeholder Management Plan: Incident and Crisis Management

766. What potential impact does the stakeholder have on the Incident and Crisis Management project?

767. Who will be collecting information?

768. Have reserves been created to address risks?

769. Do you know what your customers expectations are regarding this process?

770. Is the steering committee active in Incident and Crisis Management project oversight?

771. What are the criteria for selecting other suppliers, including subcontractors?

772. Does the system design reflect the requirements?

773. Are there standards for code development?

774. Are Incident and Crisis Management project team members involved in detailed estimating and scheduling?

775. Have all stakeholders been identified?

776. Has a sponsor been identified?

777. Have the procedures for identifying budget variances been followed?

778. Is there a formal set of procedures supporting Stakeholder Management?

779. Are regulatory inspections considered part of quality control?

780. Does the Incident and Crisis Management project have a Statement of Work?

781. After observing execution of process, is it in compliance with the documented Plan?

782. What inspection and testing is to be performed?

2.39 Change Management Plan: Incident and Crisis Management

783. How do you gain sponsors buy-in to the communication plan?

784. Who might be able to help you the most?

785. Has a training need analysis been carried out?

786. How might they respond to the message and if the response may be negative or open to misinterpretation, what else needs to be said?

787. Who might present the most resistance?

788. What are the dependencies?

789. What processes are in place to manage knowledge about the Incident and Crisis Management project?

790. Readiness -what is a successful end state?

791. What are the responsibilities assigned to each role?

792. What are the key change management success metrics?

793. Why is it important?

794. Who will be the change levers?

795. Where will the funds come from?

796. What is the worst thing that can happen if you communicate information?

797. Clearly articulate the overall business benefits of the Incident and Crisis Management project -why are you doing this now?

798. Who in the business it includes?

799. Do there need to be new channels developed?

800. Has the priority for this Incident and Crisis Management project been set by the Business Unit Management Team?

801. Who is responsible for which tasks?

802. How will the stakeholders share information and transfer knowledge?

3.0 Executing Process Group: Incident and Crisis Management

803. How do you enter durations, link tasks, and view critical path information?

804. What does it mean to take a systems view of a Incident and Crisis Management project?

805. Is activity definition the first process involved in Incident and Crisis Management project time management?

806. When will the Incident and Crisis Management project be done?

807. What areas were overlooked on this Incident and Crisis Management project?

808. Measurable - are the targets measurable?

809. How does a Incident and Crisis Management project life cycle differ from a product life cycle?

810. In what way has the program come up with innovative measures for problem-solving?

811. How can you use Microsoft Incident and Crisis Management project and Excel to assist in Incident and Crisis Management project risk management?

812. What are the main processes included in Incident and Crisis Management project quality management?

813. Have operating capacities been created and/or reinforced in partners?

814. On which process should team members spend the most time?

815. When do you share the scorecard with managers?

816. How do you prevent staff are just doing busywork to pass the time?

817. Would you rate yourself as being risk-averse, risk-neutral, or risk-seeking?

818. How could you control progress of your Incident and Crisis Management project?

819. What are the main types of contracts if you do decide to outsource?

820. Will outside resources be needed to help?

821. How is Incident and Crisis Management project performance information created and distributed?

822. Do the products created live up to the necessary quality?

3.1 Team Member Status Report: Incident and Crisis Management

823. Does your organization have the means (staff, money, contract, etc.) to produce or to acquire the product, good, or service?

824. Are the attitudes of staff regarding Incident and Crisis Management project work improving?

825. The problem with Reward & Recognition Programs is that the truly deserving people all too often get left out. How can you make it practical?

826. How much risk is involved?

827. Do you have an Enterprise Incident and Crisis Management project Management Office (EPMO)?

828. How it is to be done?

829. What is to be done?

830. When a teams productivity and success depend on collaboration and the efficient flow of information, what generally fails them?

831. Are the products of your organizations Incident and Crisis Management projects meeting customers objectives?

832. How will resource planning be done?

833. Are your organizations Incident and Crisis Management projects more successful over time?

834. Is there evidence that staff is taking a more professional approach toward management of your organizations Incident and Crisis Management projects?

835. How can you make it practical?

836. How does this product, good, or service meet the needs of the Incident and Crisis Management project and your organization as a whole?

837. What specific interest groups do you have in place?

838. Does the product, good, or service already exist within your organization?

839. Why is it to be done?

840. Does every department have to have a Incident and Crisis Management project Manager on staff?

841. Will the staff do training or is that done by a third party?

3.2 Change Request: Incident and Crisis Management

842. For which areas does this operating procedure apply?

843. Why were your requested changes rejected or not made?

844. What are the basic mechanics of the Change Advisory Board (CAB)?

845. What kind of information about the change request needs to be captured?

846. When do you create a change request?

847. Screen shots or attachments included in a Change Request?

848. What must be taken into consideration when introducing change control programs?

849. How does a team identify the discrete elements of a configuration?

850. Can static requirements change attributes like the size of the change be used to predict reliability in execution?

851. Who is responsible to authorize changes?

852. How to get changes (code) out in a timely

manner?

853. Will the change use memory to the extent that other functions will be not have sufficient memory to operate effectively?

854. Will there be a change request form in use?

855. Who has responsibility for approving and ranking changes?

856. Are you implementing itil processes?

857. What are the duties of the change control team?

858. Why do you want to have a change control system?

859. How is the change documented (format, content, storage)?

860. Have all related configuration items been properly updated?

3.3 Change Log: Incident and Crisis Management

861. Is the change request within Incident and Crisis Management project scope?

862. Is the change backward compatible without limitations?

863. Will the Incident and Crisis Management project fail if the change request is not executed?

864. Does the suggested change request seem to represent a necessary enhancement to the product?

865. Who initiated the change request?

866. Do the described changes impact on the integrity or security of the system?

867. How does this change affect scope?

868. When was the request submitted?

869. Is the requested change request a result of changes in other Incident and Crisis Management project(s)?

870. Is the change request open, closed or pending?

871. Is the submitted change a new change or a modification of a previously approved change?

872. When was the request approved?

873. How does this relate to the standards developed for specific business processes?

874. How does this change affect the timeline of the schedule?

875. Is this a mandatory replacement?

876. Where do changes come from?

877. Should a more thorough impact analysis be conducted?

878. Does the suggested change request represent a desired enhancement to the products functionality?

3.4 Decision Log: Incident and Crisis Management

879. With whom was the decision shared or considered?

880. How does an increasing emphasis on cost containment influence the strategies and tactics used?

881. Linked to original objective?

882. Does anything need to be adjusted?

883. Decision-making process; how will the team make decisions?

884. Who is the decisionmaker?

885. Meeting purpose; why does this team meet?

886. What alternatives/risks were considered?

887. How do you define success?

888. Do strategies and tactics aimed at less than full control reduce the costs of management or simply shift the cost burden?

889. How does provision of information, both in terms of content and presentation, influence acceptance of alternative strategies?

890. Which variables make a critical difference?

891. What is the line where eDiscovery ends and document review begins?

892. How consolidated and comprehensive a story can you tell by capturing currently available incident data in a central location and through a log of key decisions during an incident?

893. What is the average size of your matters in an applicable measurement?

894. What is your overall strategy for quality control / quality assurance procedures?

895. What was the rationale for the decision?

896. It becomes critical to track and periodically revisit both operational effectiveness; Are you noticing all that you need to, and are you interpreting what you see effectively?

897. Is your opponent open to a non-traditional workflow, or will it likely challenge anything you do?

898. Behaviors; what are guidelines that the team has identified that will assist them with getting the most out of team meetings?

3.5 Quality Audit: Incident and Crisis Management

899. How does your organization know that its financial management system is appropriately effective and constructive?

900. What does the organizarion look for in a Quality audit?

901. Is progress against the intentions measurable?

902. How does your organization know that its system for governing staff behaviour is appropriately effective and constructive?

903. How does your organization know that its Governance system is appropriately effective and constructive?

904. Are measuring and test equipment that have been placed out of service suitably identified and excluded from use in any device reconditioning operation?

905. Are the policies and processes, as set out in the Quality Audit Manual, properly applied?

906. How does your organization know that its processes for managing severance are appropriately effective, constructive and fair?

907. Are multiple statements on the same issue

consistent with each other?

908. What are you trying to accomplish with this audit?

909. Is the continuing professional education of key personnel account fored in detail?

910. How does your organization know that the support for its staff is appropriately effective and constructive?

911. How does your organization know that its system for ensuring a positive organizational climate is appropriately effective and constructive?

912. Are people allowed to contribute ideas?

913. Are all employees made aware of device defects which may occur from the improper performance of specific jobs?

914. Does the supplier use a formal quality system?

915. Do all staff have the necessary authority and resources to deliver what is expected of them?

916. How does your organization know that it is effectively and constructively guiding staff through to timely completion of tasks?

917. What experience do staff have in the type of work that the audit entails?

3.6 Team Directory: Incident and Crisis Management

918. How does the team resolve conflicts and ensure tasks are completed?

919. Decisions: what could be done better to improve the quality of the constructed product?

920. How will you accomplish and manage the objectives?

921. Who are the Team Members?

922. Where will the product be used and/or delivered or built when appropriate?

923. Who should receive information (all stakeholders)?

924. Who is the Sponsor?

925. Have you decided when to celebrate the Incident and Crisis Management projects completion date?

926. Does a Incident and Crisis Management project team directory list all resources assigned to the Incident and Crisis Management project?

927. Process decisions: are there any statutory or regulatory issues relevant to the timely execution of work?

928. Process decisions: which organizational elements and which individuals will be assigned management functions?

929. Process decisions: is work progressing on schedule and per contract requirements?

930. Where should the information be distributed?

931. When will you produce deliverables?

932. Who will report Incident and Crisis Management project status to all stakeholders?

933. Who will be the stakeholders on your next Incident and Crisis Management project?

934. How and in what format should information be presented?

935. When does information need to be distributed?

936. Process decisions: are contractors adequately prosecuting the work?

937. Do purchase specifications and configurations match requirements?

3.7 Team Operating Agreement: Incident and Crisis Management

938. Reimbursements: how will the team members be reimbursed for expenses and time commitments?

939. What is culture?

940. Seconds for members to respond?

941. Did you delegate tasks such as taking meeting minutes, presenting a topic and soliciting input?

942. How will you resolve conflict efficiently and respectfully?

943. Do you begin with a question to engage everyone?

944. Do you post any action items, due dates, and responsibilities on the team website?

945. Have you established procedures that team members can follow to work effectively together, such as a team operating agreement?

946. Do you brief absent members after they view meeting notes or listen to a recording?

947. Do you ask participants to close laptops and place mobile devices on silent on the table while the meeting is in progress?

948. What are the safety issues/risks that need to be addressed and/or that the team needs to consider?

949. What individual strengths does each team member bring to the group?

950. How will group handle unplanned absences?

951. Are there the right people on your team?

952. Resource allocation: how will individual team members account for time and expenses, and how will this be allocated in the team budget?

953. Does your team need access to all documents and information at all times?

954. What administrative supports will be put in place to support the team and the teams supervisor?

955. Communication protocols: how will the team communicate?

956. Did you determine the technology methods that best match the messages to be communicated?

957. Why does your organization want to participate in teaming?

3.8 Team Performance Assessment: Incident and Crisis Management

958. When a reviewer complains about method variance, what is the essence of the complaint?

959. How does Incident and Crisis Management project termination impact Incident and Crisis Management project team members?

960. Can familiarity breed backup?

961. Does more radicalness mean more perceived benefits?

962. To what degree do team members articulate the teams work approach?

963. What makes opportunities more or less obvious?

964. How do you recognize and praise members for contributions?

965. If you have received criticism from reviewers that your work suffered from method variance, what was the circumstance?

966. How much interpersonal friction is there in your team?

967. To what degree are corresponding categories of skills either actually or potentially represented across the membership?

968. Can team performance be reliably measured in simulator and live exercises using the same assessment tool?

969. To what degree does the teams work approach provide opportunity for members to engage in results-based evaluation?

970. To what degree do the goals specify concrete team work products?

971. What are teams?

972. To what degree do team members understand one anothers roles and skills?

973. To what degree will the team ensure that all members equitably share the work essential to the success of the team?

974. To what degree is the team cognizant of small wins to be celebrated along the way?

975. To what degree does the teams work approach provide opportunity for members to engage in fact-based problem solving?

976. To what degree will new and supplemental skills be introduced as the need is recognized?

977. If you have criticized someones work for method variance in your role as reviewer, what was the circumstance?

3.9 Team Member Performance Assessment: Incident and Crisis Management

978. What resources do you need?

979. Who should attend?

980. How do you determine which data are the most important to use, analyze, or review?

981. How are performance measures and associated incentives developed?

982. How is assessment information achieved, stored?

983. Are any governance changes sufficient to impact achievement?

984. For what period of time is a member rated?

985. What happens if a team member receives a Rating of Unsatisfactory?

986. Which training platform formats (i.e., mobile, virtual, videogame-based) were implemented in your effort(s)?

987. How is your organizations Strategic Management System tied to performance measurement?

988. To what degree can team members frequently and easily communicate with one another?

989. How do you currently account for your results in the teams achievement?

990. What are the basic principles and objectives of performance measurement and assessment?

991. To what degree are sub-teams possible or necessary?

992. What variables that affect team members achievement are within your control?

993. Is it clear how goals will be accomplished?

994. Did training work?

995. How often should assessments be conducted?

996. In what areas would you like to concentrate your knowledge and resources?

997. How often are assessments to be conducted?

3.10 Issue Log: Incident and Crisis Management

998. Is the issue log kept in a safe place?

999. How were past initiatives successful?

1000. Do you have members of your team responsible for certain stakeholders?

1001. How do you manage communications?

1002. How is this initiative related to other portfolios, programs, or Incident and Crisis Management projects?

1003. Are the Incident and Crisis Management project issues uniquely identified, including to which product they refer?

1004. Who do you turn to if you have questions?

1005. What is the impact on the risks?

1006. What are the typical contents?

1007. Do you feel a register helps?

1008. How much time does it take to do it?

1009. Do you feel more overwhelmed by stakeholders?

1010. Is access to the Issue Log controlled?

1011. What is the status of the issue?

1012. Is there an important stakeholder who is actively opposed and will not receive messages?

1013. Who have you worked with in past, similar initiatives?

1014. Why do you manage communications?

4.0 Monitoring and Controlling Process Group: Incident and Crisis Management

1015. How many more potential communications channels were introduced by the discovery of the new stakeholders?

1016. How can you make your needs known?

1017. How was the program set-up initiated?

1018. Did the Incident and Crisis Management project team have enough people to execute the Incident and Crisis Management project plan?

1019. Feasibility: how much money, time, and effort can you put into this?

1020. Were decisions made in a timely manner?

1021. Contingency planning. if a risk event occurs, what will you do?

1022. Where is the Risk in the Incident and Crisis Management project?

1023. How is agile Incident and Crisis Management project management done?

1024. What are the goals of the program?

1025. How well did you do?

1026. If a risk event occurs, what will you do?

1027. What input will you be required to provide the Incident and Crisis Management project team?

1028. User: who wants the information and what are they interested in?

1029. Where is the Risk in the Incident and Crisis Management project?

1030. Is the verbiage used appropriate and understandable?

1031. Based on your Incident and Crisis Management project communication management plan, what worked well?

4.1 Project Performance Report: Incident and Crisis Management

1032. To what degree will the approach capitalize on and enhance the skills of all team members in a manner that takes into consideration other demands on members of the team?

1033. To what degree are the structures of the formal organization consistent with the behaviors in the informal organization?

1034. To what degree can the team ensure that all members are individually and jointly accountable for the teams purpose, goals, approach, and work-products?

1035. How will procurement be coordinated with other Incident and Crisis Management project aspects, such as scheduling and performance reporting?

1036. What is in it for you?

1037. To what degree are fresh input and perspectives systematically caught and added (for example, through information and analysis, new members, and senior sponsors)?

1038. What degree are the relative importance and priority of the goals clear to all team members?

1039. To what degree will the team adopt a concrete,

clearly understood, and agreed-upon approach that will result in achievement of the teams goals?

1040. To what degree are the demands of the task compatible with and converge with the relationships of the informal organization?

1041. To what degree are the teams goals and objectives clear, simple, and measurable?

1042. To what degree is the information network consistent with the structure of the formal organization?

1043. To what degree do individual skills and abilities match task demands?

1044. To what degree do members articulate the goals beyond the team membership?

1045. To what degree does the teams purpose contain themes that are particularly meaningful and memorable?

1046. To what degree can team members meet frequently enough to accomplish the teams ends?

1047. To what degree does the informal organization make use of individual resources and meet individual needs?

1048. To what degree can the cognitive capacity of individuals accommodate the flow of information?

4.2 Variance Analysis: Incident and Crisis Management

1049. Are procedures for variance analysis documented and consistently applied at the control account level and selected WBS and organizational levels at least monthly as a routine task?

1050. Are the wbs and organizational levels for application of the Incident and Crisis Management projected overhead costs identified?

1051. What business event causes fluctuations?

1052. What is your organizations rationale for sharing expenses and services between business segments?

1053. How do you evaluate the impact of schedule changes, work around, et?

1054. Does the accounting system provide a basis for auditing records of direct costs chargeable to the contract?

1055. Are control accounts opened and closed based on the start and completion of work contained therein?

1056. What is the incurrence of actual indirect costs in excess of budgets, by element of expense?

1057. Did an existing competitor change strategy?

1058. What types of services and expense are shared between business segments?

1059. Is data disseminated to the contractors management timely, accurate, and usable?

1060. Is work properly classified as measured effort, LOE, or apportioned effort and appropriately separated?

1061. Can process improvements lead to unfavorable variances?

1062. Are authorized changes being incorporated in a timely manner?

1063. How does the use of a single conversion element (rather than the traditional labor and overhead elements) affect standard costing?

1064. What causes selling price variance?

1065. Did a new competitor enter the market?

1066. Did your organization lose existing customers and/or gain new customers?

1067. Are the actual costs used for variance analysis reconcilable with data from the accounting system?

4.3 Earned Value Status: Incident and Crisis Management

1068. How much is it going to cost by the finish?

1069. Are you hitting your Incident and Crisis Management projects targets?

1070. What is the unit of forecast value?

1071. Where is evidence-based earned value in your organization reported?

1072. Where are your problem areas?

1073. How does this compare with other Incident and Crisis Management projects?

1074. If earned value management (EVM) is so good in determining the true status of a Incident and Crisis Management project and Incident and Crisis Management project its completion, why is it that hardly any one uses it in information systems related Incident and Crisis Management projects?

1075. Validation is a process of ensuring that the developed system will actually achieve the stakeholders desired outcomes; Are you building the right product? What do you validate?

1076. Verification is a process of ensuring that the developed system satisfies the stakeholders agreements and specifications; Are you building the product right? What do you verify?

1077. Earned value can be used in almost any Incident and Crisis Management project situation and in almost any Incident and Crisis Management project environment. it may be used on large Incident and Crisis Management projects, medium sized Incident and Crisis Management projects, tiny Incident and Crisis Management projects (in cut-down form), complex and simple Incident and Crisis Management projects and in any market sector. some people, of course, know all about earned value, they have used it for years - but perhaps not as effectively as they could have?

1078. When is it going to finish?

4.4 Risk Audit: Incident and Crisis Management

1079. Does the customer have a solid idea of what is required?

1080. What expertise do auditors need to generate effective business-level risk assessments, and to what extent do auditors currently possess the already stated attributes?

1081. Are formal technical reviews part of this process?

1082. What are the costs associated with late delivery or a defective product?

1083. What programmatic and Fiscal information is being collected and analyzed?

1084. Are contracts reviewed before renewal?

1085. Are corresponding safety and risk management policies posted for all to see?

1086. What are the boundaries of the auditors responsibility for policing management fidelity?

1087. How do you govern assets?

1088. Is safety information provided to all involved?

1089. Does the customer understand the process?

1090. Have permissions or required permits to use facilities managed by other parties been obtained?

1091. Who audits the auditor?

1092. Do you ensure the recommended rules of play and protocols are followed for your activity?

1093. Is Incident and Crisis Management project scope stable?

1094. Have you considered the health and safety of everyone in your organization and do you meet work health and safety regulations?

1095. Level of preparation and skill?

1096. How effective are your risk controls?

1097. Are end-users enthusiastically committed to the Incident and Crisis Management project and the system/product to be built?

4.5 Contractor Status Report: Incident and Crisis Management

1098. How does the proposed individual meet each requirement?

1099. What are the minimum and optimal bandwidth requirements for the proposed solution?

1100. What was the budget or estimated cost for your organizations services?

1101. What was the overall budget or estimated cost?

1102. Who can list a Incident and Crisis Management project as organization experience, your organization or a previous employee of your organization?

1103. What was the final actual cost?

1104. What process manages the contracts?

1105. Are there contractual transfer concerns?

1106. Describe how often regular updates are made to the proposed solution. Are corresponding regular updates included in the standard maintenance plan?

1107. How long have you been using the services?

1108. How is risk transferred?

1109. What was the actual budget or estimated cost

for your organizations services?

1110. If applicable; describe your standard schedule for new software version releases. Are new software version releases included in the standard maintenance plan?

1111. What is the average response time for answering a support call?

4.6 Formal Acceptance: Incident and Crisis Management

1112. Was the Incident and Crisis Management project work done on time, within budget, and according to specification?

1113. Did the Incident and Crisis Management project achieve its MOV?

1114. What lessons were learned about your Incident and Crisis Management project management methodology?

1115. Does it do what Incident and Crisis Management project team said it would?

1116. Is formal acceptance of the Incident and Crisis Management project product documented and distributed?

1117. Was the sponsor/customer satisfied?

1118. Do you buy pre-configured systems or build your own configuration?

1119. What are the requirements against which to test, Who will execute?

1120. What is the Acceptance Management Process?

1121. Was the client satisfied with the Incident and Crisis Management project results?

1122. What features, practices, and processes proved to be strengths or weaknesses?

1123. Do you perform formal acceptance or burn-in tests?

1124. Was the Incident and Crisis Management project managed well?

1125. Do you buy-in installation services?

1126. General estimate of the costs and times to complete the Incident and Crisis Management project?

1127. Was business value realized?

1128. Who supplies data?

1129. Was the Incident and Crisis Management project goal achieved?

1130. How does your team plan to obtain formal acceptance on your Incident and Crisis Management project?

1131. Did the Incident and Crisis Management project manager and team act in a professional and ethical manner?

5.0 Closing Process Group: Incident and Crisis Management

1132. What is the amount of funding and what Incident and Crisis Management project phases are funded?

1133. Will the Incident and Crisis Management project deliverable(s) replace a current asset or group of assets?

1134. Was the user/client satisfied with the end product?

1135. Does the close educate others to improve performance?

1136. What could have been improved?

1137. Did you do things well?

1138. When will the Incident and Crisis Management project be done?

1139. Who are the Incident and Crisis Management project stakeholders?

1140. How well did the chosen processes produce the expected results?

1141. Were risks identified and mitigated?

1142. Did the Incident and Crisis Management project

team have enough people to execute the Incident and Crisis Management project plan?

1143. Is this a follow-on to a previous Incident and Crisis Management project?

1144. What is the overall risk of the Incident and Crisis Management project to your organization?

1145. Did the delivered product meet the specified requirements and goals of the Incident and Crisis Management project?

1146. What areas does the group agree are the biggest success on the Incident and Crisis Management project?

1147. Were the outcomes different from the already stated planned?

1148. Can the lesson learned be replicated?

5.1 Procurement Audit: Incident and Crisis Management

1149. Do your organizations policies promote and/or safeguard fair competition?

1150. Have the funding arrangements been agreed where payments take place over several financial periods?

1151. Are copies of policies made available to staff members involved in budget preparation and administration?

1152. Does your organization make sources of information beyond the tender documents equally available for all the candidates?

1153. Are there performance targets on value for money obtained and cost savings?

1154. If the expert was allowed to submit a tender, was all the relevant information the expert had gained from his earlier involvement made available to the other bidders?

1155. Is a log maintained over the use of signature plates?

1156. Is there a formal program of inservice training for personnel in the business management function?

1157. Is there a legal authority for the procurement

Incident and Crisis Management project?

1158. Are outsourcing and Public Private Partnerships considered as alternatives to in-house work?

1159. Did your organization calculate the contract value accurately?

1160. Does your organization have an overall procurement strategy and/or policy?

1161. Are required quality and service standards set?

1162. Are bank accounts reconciled by an individual independent of the disbursement responsibilities?

1163. Does the strategy discus the best manner of purchase, considering the types of goods and services needed?

1164. Was your organization specific about the nature and scope of the performance before launching the procurement process?

1165. Is a cost/benefit analysis, a cost/effectiveness or a financial analysis considering life-cycle costs performed and is the funding of the procurement guaranteed?

1166. Are the established budget and timetable (milestones) respected?

1167. Were the specifications of the contract determined free from influence of particular interests of consultants, experts or other economic operators?

1168. Are the financial and business records of your organization stored in a secure fire resistant place?

5.2 Contract Close-Out: Incident and Crisis Management

1169. Was the contract type appropriate?

1170. How is the contracting office notified of the automatic contract close-out?

1171. Why Outsource?

1172. How does it work?

1173. Change in circumstances?

1174. Has each contract been audited to verify acceptance and delivery?

1175. Have all contracts been completed?

1176. Have all contract records been included in the Incident and Crisis Management project archives?

1177. What is capture management?

1178. Have all contracts been closed?

1179. Change in attitude or behavior?

1180. Parties: who is involved?

1181. What happens to the recipient of services?

1182. Are the signers the authorized officials?

1183. Was the contract complete without requiring numerous changes and revisions?

1184. Have all acceptance criteria been met prior to final payment to contractors?

1185. How/when used ?

1186. Parties: Authorized?

1187. Was the contract sufficiently clear so as not to result in numerous disputes and misunderstandings?

1188. Change in knowledge?

5.3 Project or Phase Close-Out: Incident and Crisis Management

1189. Is the lesson based on actual Incident and Crisis Management project experience rather than on independent research?

1190. What are the marketing communication needs for each stakeholder?

1191. How often did each stakeholder need an update?

1192. What information is each stakeholder group interested in?

1193. What were the desired outcomes?

1194. If you were the Incident and Crisis Management project sponsor, how would you determine which Incident and Crisis Management project team(s) and/or individuals deserve recognition?

1195. What stakeholder group needs, expectations, and interests are being met by the Incident and Crisis Management project?

1196. Is there a clear cause and effect between the activity and the lesson learned?

1197. What was expected from each stakeholder?

1198. What hierarchical authority does the

stakeholder have in your organization?

1199. Who exerted influence that has positively affected or negatively impacted the Incident and Crisis Management project?

1200. Does the lesson educate others to improve performance?

1201. What is the information level of detail required for each stakeholder?

1202. What are the mandatory communication needs for each stakeholder?

1203. What benefits or impacts does the stakeholder group expect to obtain as a result of the Incident and Crisis Management project?

1204. Planned remaining costs?

5.4 Lessons Learned: Incident and Crisis Management

1205. How useful do individuals find communications?

1206. How effectively and timely was your organizational change impact identified and planned for?

1207. What is in the future?

1208. Will the information remain current?

1209. Are the lessons more complex and multivariate?

1210. How effective were the communications materials in providing and orienting team members about the details of the Incident and Crisis Management project?

1211. How many government and contractor personnel are authorized for the Incident and Crisis Management project?

1212. Are there any data that you have overlooked in identifying lessons?

1213. What other questions should you have asked?

1214. Was the schedule met?

1215. How well were Incident and Crisis Management

project issues communicated throughout your involvement in the Incident and Crisis Management project?

1216. How well is the build process working?

1217. What were the problems encountered in the Incident and Crisis Management project-functional area relationship, why, and how could they be fixed?

1218. Why does your organization need a lessons learned (LL) capability?

1219. What is the impact of tax policy?

1220. How efficient and effective were Incident and Crisis Management project team meetings?

1221. Who needs to learn lessons?

1222. What is the fiscal dependency?

1223. How useful was your testing?

1224. How often do communications get lost?

Index

abilities 249
ability   33, 84
absences   239
absent 94, 238
acceptable   58, 89, 96, 200
acceptance   9, 111, 149, 232, 258-259, 265-266
accepted   109, 191, 216
accepting   178, 185
access 4, 10-12, 25, 63, 148, 216, 239, 245
accomplish   10, 82, 107, 128, 136, 146, 168, 219, 235-236, 249
according   38-39, 258
account   30, 235, 239, 243, 250
accounted   82
accounting   250-251
accounts   198, 250, 263
accrue 147
accuracy   53, 165
accurate   12, 121, 251
accurately   263
achievable   110
achieve   10, 70, 78, 106, 113, 129, 168, 196-197, 203, 211, 214, 252, 258
achieved   20, 81, 83, 129, 134, 201, 242, 259
achieving   142
acquire   226
acquired   178
across 240
action 45, 49, 95, 97, 103, 158, 177, 209, 238
actionable   57
actions 20, 50, 97, 101, 106, 121, 198, 208-209
active 202, 220
actively   245
activities   22-23, 35, 80, 92, 103, 108, 147, 164, 166-168, 172, 176, 178, 181, 186, 194, 200, 209, 214
activity 5-6, 31, 40, 166-170, 172, 174, 177-178, 183, 186-187, 216, 224, 255, 267
actual 31, 50, 161-162, 250-251, 256, 267
actually   37, 67, 88, 240, 252
adapted   142
addition   200

271

additional   43, 66-68, 72, 148, 188, 198
additions   101
address   1, 87, 136, 141, 147, 164, 219-220
addressed   174, 239
addressing   33, 109
adequate   145, 154-155, 206
adequately   43, 141, 161, 195, 237
adhered   161-162
Adjust 94-95
adjusted   98, 232
adopters   205
advance   162
advantage   1, 70, 119
advantages   130
adverse   198
advise 2
Advisory   219, 228
affect 62, 69-70, 122, 127, 152, 155, 157, 178, 192, 208, 212, 230-231, 243, 251
affected   123, 125, 140, 184-185, 214, 268
affecting   14, 21
afford 206, 208
affordable   87
against33, 98, 100, 146, 161, 234, 258
agendas   117
agents 197
agreed   184-185, 262
agreement   8, 128, 178, 238
agreements   216, 252
agrees 121, 196
aiming 129, 203
alerts   96
aligned   21
alleged   3
alliance   79
allocate   105
allocated   51, 129, 162, 239
allocation   239
allowable   46
allowed   2, 126, 176, 235, 262
allows 12, 173, 183
almost 253
already   195, 200, 227, 254, 261

272

always 12
amount   19, 260
amplify 66, 119
analysis   4, 8, 12-13, 47, 50, 55, 58, 63-64, 66-67, 72-73, 86, 139, 178, 188, 195, 202, 211, 214, 219, 222, 231, 248, 250-251, 263
analytics   51
analyze   4, 60, 65, 68, 242
analyzed   46, 96, 198, 213, 254
analyzes   146
annual 190
another   168, 212, 242
anothers   241
answer 13-14, 18, 29, 45, 60, 76, 92, 105, 154
answered   28, 44, 59, 75, 91, 103, 132
answering   13, 170, 257
anticipate   155
anyone   41, 94, 122-123
anything   165, 174, 194, 206, 232-233
appear   3
applicable   13, 94, 149, 233, 257
applied   80, 184, 192, 234, 250
appointed   37, 41
appreciate   201
approach   48, 76, 88, 113, 130, 139, 164, 187, 227, 240-241, 248-249
approached   122
approaches   85, 141, 205
approval   43, 107
approvals   158
approved   30, 149, 152, 158, 164, 190, 202, 230-231
approving   152, 229
architect   155
Architects   10
archived   190
archives   265
around 117, 121, 250
arrest   109
articulate   223, 240, 249
asking 3, 10, 178, 190, 196-197
aspects   170, 248
assess   27, 35, 87, 103, 106, 173, 178, 211
assessed   89, 207
assessing   95

273

assessment 7-8, 11-12, 23, 27, 146, 165, 210-211, 216, 240-243
assets 48, 254, 260
assign 24
assigned 31, 35, 144, 154, 159, 164-165, 168, 198, 216, 222, 236-237
Assignment 6, 198
assist 11, 70, 83, 93, 106, 189, 198, 224, 233
assistance 30, 41
assistant 10
associated 242, 254
Assumption 5, 157
assurance 164, 185, 193, 203, 233
attached 180
attainable 31
attained 206
attempted 41
attempting 93
attend 18, 242
attendance 41
attendant 91
attended 1, 41
attending 211
attention 14, 114
attitude 265
attitudes 226
attributes 5, 115, 150, 168, 195, 228, 254
audited 165, 265
auditing 95, 111, 250
auditor 255
auditors 193, 254
audits 193, 255
author 3, 148
authority 62, 134, 200, 204, 235, 262, 267
authorize 228
authorized 144-145, 161, 198, 251, 265-266, 269
automatic 265
available 20, 27, 34, 43, 49, 67, 84, 93, 112, 127, 135, 146, 166, 172, 178, 183, 192, 195, 206, 211, 214, 233, 262
Average 14, 28, 44, 59, 75, 91, 103, 132, 180, 202, 233, 257
background 12
backup 240
backward 230
balance 200

balanced 88
bandwidth 256
barriers 111
baseline 6, 116, 145, 164, 190
baselined 184
baselines 36, 40
basics 120
because 2
become 105, 107, 130-131, 149, 152
becomes 206, 233
before 1-2, 12, 41, 94, 165-166, 172, 207-208, 254, 263
beginning 4, 17, 28, 44, 59, 75, 91, 104, 132
begins 233
behavior 265
behaviors 48, 201, 233, 248
behaviour 234
behind 2
belief 13, 18, 29, 45, 60, 76, 92, 105-106
believable 110
believe 2, 106, 121
benchmark 195
benefit 3, 21, 25, 51, 55, 93, 263
benefits 21, 45, 51-52, 72, 105-106, 109, 120, 124, 129, 136, 141, 147, 151, 172, 206, 223, 240, 268
better 10, 30, 52, 76, 140, 166, 180-181, 189, 194, 214, 236
between 64, 134, 152, 165, 178, 185, 193, 204, 250-251, 267
beyond 249, 262
bidders 149, 262
biggest 52, 88, 187, 261
blinding 71
bother 47
bottleneck 167
bounce 67
boundaries 36, 254
bounds 36
Breakdown 5-6, 154, 159-160, 175
briefed 37
brings 33
broken 70
budget 2, 99, 103, 127, 144, 167, 182-184, 190-191, 198, 209, 213, 220, 239, 256, 258, 262-263
Budgeted 50, 199
budgets 26, 111, 161-162, 198, 201, 250

building   20, 97, 136, 141, 175, 252
burden 232
burn-in 259
business   2, 10, 12, 24, 26, 51-52, 54, 57, 71, 74, 84-85, 89, 114, 116, 119, 122, 124, 127, 129, 131, 137, 150-151, 154, 161, 187, 191, 203, 223, 231, 250-251, 259, 262, 264
busywork   225
buy-in 130, 222, 259
calculate   178, 195, 263
calendar   178
calibrated   192
candidates   262
cannot 172, 182
capability   27, 146, 270
capable   10, 37
capacities   225
capacity   20, 27, 79, 141, 249
capital 119
capitalize   66, 248
capture   57, 99, 265
captured   47, 129, 147, 150, 164, 184, 202, 228
capturing   233
career 152, 200
carried 73, 214, 222
catching   1
categories   210, 240
category   40
caught 248
caused   3
causes 45, 47, 51-52, 54, 60, 63-64, 72, 97, 162, 177, 250-251
causing   21
celebrate   86, 236
celebrated   241
center 50
central 233
centrally   88
certain 244
Certified   164, 216
challenge   10, 233
challenges   108, 170
champion   39
champions   196
chances   206, 212

276

change 7-8, 18, 28, 32, 54, 61, 65-66, 68, 74, 80, 88, 90, 127, 137-138, 148, 155, 169, 172, 182, 184, 186, 197, 202, 209, 222, 228-231, 250, 265-266, 269
changed 22, 32, 77, 96, 111, 183, 186, 188, 208
changes 32, 35, 39, 86, 91, 94, 101, 108, 111, 155, 161-162, 175, 178, 183-185, 190, 192, 228-231, 242, 250-251, 266
changing 94, 121, 140
channel 134
channels 118, 123, 223, 246
charge 112, 118
chargeable 250
charged 50
charges 186
charter 4, 29, 44, 80, 136-137
charters 43
charts 63, 183
cheaper 52
checked 65, 93, 97, 99, 150
checklists 11, 217
choice 40, 116
choose 13, 81
chosen 141-142, 215, 260
circumvent 24
claimed 3
clarify 109
classes 202
classified 251
clearly 13, 18, 25, 29, 32, 41, 44-45, 60, 64, 76, 89, 92, 105, 151, 203, 223, 249
client 118, 258, 260
clients 20, 40
climate 235
closed 101, 230, 250, 265
closely 12
Close-Out 9, 219, 265, 267
closest 128
Closing 9, 72, 260
coaches 32, 35, 197
cognitive 249
cognizant 241
coherent 147, 202
colleague 113
colleagues 109, 117, 181

collect 64, 103, 188, 197
collected	30, 35, 63, 66, 71-72, 254
collecting	220
collection	63, 196
combine	84
coming	61
Command	117
commit	207, 216
commitment	101
committed	67, 210, 255
committee	157, 202, 219-220
common	182, 187, 204, 216, 218
community	180-181, 188-189, 193, 209
companies	3, 98
company	1-2, 10, 52, 70, 113-114, 116, 119, 121-122, 131
compare	73, 89, 193, 252
compared	162, 212
comparing	85
comparison	13
compatible	230, 249
compelling	33
competing	49
competitor	2, 250-251
complains	240
complaint	240
complete	3, 11, 13, 23, 42-43, 106, 145, 165, 167-168, 170, 180-181, 194, 201, 211, 259, 266
completed	14, 32-33, 40-41, 162, 172, 178, 216, 236, 265
completely	1, 116, 180
completing	123, 159, 172
completion	40, 44, 134, 162, 191, 235-236, 250, 252
complex	10, 113, 183, 253, 269
complexity	22, 46, 48
compliance	1, 28, 49, 58, 61, 221
comply	136, 178
component	194
components	164, 185, 211
compute	14
computing	116
concept	82
concepts	158
concern	47, 79, 118
concerned	18

concerns	2, 20, 22, 112, 128, 256
concrete	78, 241, 248
condition	101
conditions	99, 130, 144
conduct	193
conducted	146, 165, 231, 243
confident	173
confirm	13
conflict	238
conflicts	177, 194, 236
conform	192
conjure	150
connecting	106
consider	21, 24, 178, 239
considered	20-21, 47, 218, 221, 232, 255, 263
considers	70
consist	161
consistent	44, 59, 65, 95, 161, 235, 248-249
constantly	1
Constraint	5, 157
consult	1, 126
consultant	1-2, 10, 186
consulted	123
consulting	2, 52
consumers	111
contact	10, 147
contacts	113
contain	19, 101, 249
contained	3, 250
contains	11
content	37, 145, 229, 232
contents	3-4, 11, 244
context	36, 42
continual	101-102
continuing	235
Continuity	57, 170
continuous	69, 80
contract	9, 161-162, 177, 198, 218, 226, 237, 250, 263, 265-266
contracted	187
contractor	8, 134, 155, 187, 198, 256, 269
contracts	43, 140, 225, 254, 256, 265
contribute	235

control 4, 36, 59, 61, 92, 96, 98-101, 134, 139, 148, 154-155, 161, 165, 183, 185, 188, 198, 221, 225, 228-229, 232-233, 243, 250
controlled 61, 208, 245
controls 19, 69, 78, 86, 91, 93, 96-99, 103, 173, 214, 255
convention 131
converge 249
conversion 251
convey 3, 123
convince 199
cooperate 189
copies 262
Copyright 3
corporate 2
correct 45, 92, 126, 146
corrective 50, 97, 177
correspond 11-12
costing 55, 251
counting 182
course 32, 253
coverage 101
covering 11, 95, 200
coworker 118
crashing 172
create 21, 119, 130, 154, 177, 228
created 66, 95, 138, 144, 147, 185, 209, 220, 225
creating 10, 52, 141, 156
creative 26
creativity 77
credible 189
Crisis 3-9, 11-16, 18-44, 46-67, 69-104, 106-142, 144-150, 152, 154-161, 164-168, 170-194, 196, 198-212, 214, 216-228, 230, 232, 234, 236-238, 240, 242, 244, 246-248, 250, 252-256, 258-263, 265, 267-270
criteria 4, 7, 11-12, 31, 34, 40, 81, 83, 87, 95, 119-120, 133-134, 144, 149, 152, 177, 188, 218, 220, 266
CRITERION 4, 18, 29, 45, 60, 76, 92, 105, 146
critical 30, 37-38, 66, 97, 124, 142, 147, 167, 170, 218, 224, 233
criticism 240
criticized 241
crucial 66, 170
crystal 13
culture 35, 184, 201, 212, 238

current 40, 45, 57, 64, 72-73, 77, 99, 106, 113, 119-120, 123, 158, 161, 178, 184, 212-213, 260, 269
currently 38, 114, 233, 243, 254
custom 23
customer 23, 30, 35-36, 39, 43, 78, 93, 108, 112-113, 116, 118, 136-137, 150, 155, 194, 207, 210, 212, 254, 258
customers 3, 20, 32, 34, 38, 53-54, 57, 72-73, 100, 107, 114-115, 120, 124, 126, 128, 130-131, 150-151, 155, 157, 164, 170, 214, 220, 226, 251
customized 2
cut-down 253
damage 3, 85, 206-207
danger 110
Dashboard 11
dashboards 101
day-to-day 102, 106
deadlines 20
dealing 24
deceitful 118
decide 87, 192, 200-201, 225
decided 81, 236
deciding 130
decision 8, 53, 80-81, 83-84, 88, 208, 232-233
decisions 76, 83, 86-87, 91, 102-103, 147, 199-200, 232-233, 236-237, 246
dedicated 10
deeper 13
defect 202
defective 254
defects 235
define 4, 29, 34-35, 41, 68, 71, 77, 160, 180, 232
defined 13, 18-19, 26, 29, 32-37, 40-41, 43-45, 60-61, 64, 76, 92, 105, 154, 158-159, 161, 177, 183-184, 193, 200, 203
defines 23, 33, 37, 175
defining 10, 126, 154, 185
definite 101
definition 19, 25, 31, 33, 38, 177, 224
degree 240-243, 248-249
-degree 2
delaying 49
delays 53, 167, 181
delegate 238
delegated 37

delete 186
deletions 101
deliver 20, 38, 78, 124, 129, 180, 187, 189, 235
delivered 57, 120, 183, 191, 236, 261
delivers 175
delivery 25, 54, 120, 130, 143, 173, 254, 265
demand 119, 211
demands 212, 248-249
department 10, 119, 227
depend 226
dependency 270
dependent 120
depends 114
depict 173
deploy 95, 127-128
deployed 96
deploying 52
deployment 55
derive 95, 171
Describe 24, 146, 152, 256-257
described 3, 151, 161, 190, 230
describes 178
describing 32, 178
deserve 267
deserving 226
design 12, 62, 73, 79, 86, 113, 141, 148, 157, 198, 211, 220
designed 10, 12, 67, 79, 89
designing 10
desired 43, 64, 90, 175, 231, 252, 267
detail 48, 169, 180, 235, 268
detailed 64, 66, 149, 157, 162, 166, 184, 202, 216, 220
details 48, 115, 269
detect 99, 195
detention 109
determine 12, 127, 166, 178, 188, 211, 218, 239, 242, 267
determined 71, 127, 165, 196-197, 210, 263
determines 187
detracting 112
develop 76, 78-79, 84, 88, 159-160
developed 12, 33, 42-44, 51, 80, 83, 157, 190, 223, 231, 242, 252
developer 210
developers 148

developing   68, 79
deviation   178
device 234-235
devices   238
diagram   6, 51, 53, 63, 172-173, 182
diagrams   47
Dictionary   5, 161
differ   178, 183, 224
difference   142, 155, 165, 233
different   10, 23, 30, 37-39, 63, 70, 115, 127, 141, 145, 158, 165, 184, 261
difficult 72, 166, 172, 176, 190
dilemma   124
direct   161-162, 250
direction   32, 52
directly 3, 72-73, 110, 204
Directory   8, 236
Disagree   13, 18, 29, 45, 60, 76, 92, 105
disaster   57, 125, 182
disclosure   98
discovery   246
discrete   161, 228
discus   263
discussion   131
displayed   30, 61, 166, 181
disposed   190
disputes   266
disqualify   67
disruptive   74
Divided   28, 37, 44, 59, 75, 91, 103, 132
document   12, 38, 148, 151, 154, 164, 193, 233
documented   40, 86, 89, 94, 96-97, 150, 155, 157-158, 185, 190, 201, 217, 221, 229, 250, 258
documents   10, 239, 262
domains   90
dormant   113
Driver   69
drivers   49, 71
drives   53
driving   105, 131
duration   6, 109, 142, 160, 173, 177-178, 180
durations   31, 224

during 25, 32, 86, 117, 145, 147, 168, 174, 192, 210-212, 214, 217, 233
duties 125, 199, 229
dynamic 48
dynamics 39
eagerly 2
earlier 126, 262
earned 8, 178, 199, 252-253
easily 242
economic 263
economical 117
economy 84, 178
eDiscovery 233
edition 11
editorial 3
educate 260, 268
educated 1
education 25, 94, 235
effect 165, 209, 267
effective 18, 108, 127, 129, 150, 234-235, 254-255, 269-270
effects 55, 171
efficiency 61, 100, 218
efficient 54, 89, 226, 270
effort 37, 47, 56, 107, 164, 199, 242, 246, 251
efforts 41, 82, 106, 110, 112
either 240
elected 83
electronic 3
element 161-162, 250-251
elements 12, 63, 99, 127, 147, 197-198, 202, 228, 237, 251
elicit 196
embarking 33
embeddings 195
emergency 25, 111, 118, 121
emergent 48
emerging 1, 69, 93
emphasis 232
employee 87, 256
employees 20, 28, 73, 109-110, 114, 193, 235
employers 138
empower 10
enable 74
enablers 119

encourage 77, 99, 218
endure 186
end-users 210, 255
energy 1
engage 204, 238, 241
engagement 57, 138, 204
enhance 100, 178, 248
enhancing 92
enough 10, 114-115, 120, 148, 152, 165, 206, 246, 249, 261
ensure 31, 33, 73-74, 91, 108, 111, 124, 129, 149, 158, 186, 192, 196, 236, 241, 248, 255
ensures 124
ensuring 12, 129, 235, 252
entail 58
entails 235
Enterprise 226
entities 50
entity 3
envisaged 143
equally 262
equipment 25, 27, 135, 192, 234
equipped 34
equitably 37, 241
errors 114
especially 81
essence 240
essential 83, 241
essentials 110
establish 76, 95, 188, 210
estimate 46-47, 58, 145, 181, 259
estimated 40, 44, 47, 122, 188-189, 209, 256
estimates 6, 33, 50, 65, 157, 162, 177-178, 186, 190, 198
estimating 6, 180, 184, 188-189, 202, 216, 220
estimation 84, 178
estimator 186
etcetera 46, 130
ethical 121, 259
ethnic 119
evaluate 77, 86, 88, 162, 250
evaluating 81, 83
evaluation 82, 91, 99, 144, 177, 218-219, 241
events 18, 78, 82, 212
everyday 1, 73

everyone 37, 43, 196, 238, 255
evidence 13, 49, 218, 227
evolution 45
evolve 103
exactly 201
examined 41
Example 4, 11, 15, 25, 67, 248
examples 10-11
exceed 160, 173, 183
exceeding 57
excellence 10, 31
excellent 52
excess 162, 250
excessive 164
excited 1
exclude 86
excluded 234
execute 246, 258, 261
executed 230
Executing 7, 224
execution 95, 192, 221, 228, 236
executive 10, 118
executives 124
Exercise 25, 173
exercises 241
exerted 268
existence 161
existing 12, 106, 144, 155, 250-251
expect 107, 180, 191, 268
expected 21, 31, 141, 235, 260, 267
expend 56
expense 250-251
expenses 238-239, 250
experience 29, 113, 127-128, 181, 186, 206-207, 211, 235, 256, 267
experiment 120
expert 41, 262
expertise 84, 254
experts 41, 212, 263
explained 12
explicitly 109
explore 63, 213
exposures 79

expressed 144
extensive 2
extent 13, 18, 22, 25, 42, 83, 141-142, 229, 254
external 1-2, 41, 109, 195, 205
facilitate 13, 25, 68, 101
facilities 255
facing 24, 124, 210
fact-based 241
factor 149
factors 47, 79, 112, 172, 189
failed 46
failure 50, 130-131
fairly 37
familiar 11
fashion 3, 31
feasible 58, 70, 107, 188, 209
feature 12
features 211, 259
feedback 35-36, 46
feeling 1
fidelity 254
finalize 219
finalized 15
financial 58, 61, 65, 72, 116, 124, 141, 206, 208, 234, 262-264
fingertips 12
finish 166, 171, 173, 252-253
fiscal 254, 270
focused 48
follow 96, 113, 122, 141, 172, 177, 238
followed 40, 165, 202, 220, 255
following 11, 13, 154, 196
follow-on 261
follow-up 143
for--and 98
forecast 252
forefront 117
foresee 170
forever 111
forget 12
formal 9, 113, 221, 235, 248-249, 254, 258-259, 262
formally 157, 177, 191, 208, 216
format 12, 229, 237

formats 242
formed 35
formula 14, 107
Formulate 29
forward 2, 109, 131
foster 111, 115
framework 106, 197
freaky 115
frequency 34, 95, 111, 196
frequently 48, 56, 242, 249
friction 240
friend 113, 124-125
friends 2
frontiers 88
fulfill 125
full-blown 49
full-scale 86
function 187, 262
functions 34, 74, 108, 120, 150-151, 154, 200, 229, 237
funded 190, 260
funding 106, 114, 157, 260, 262-263
further 11, 198, 208
future 10, 53, 94, 102, 131, 139, 142, 144, 269
gained 2, 68, 101-102, 262
gather 13, 30, 32, 34-36, 38-39, 42, 45, 63, 70-71
gathered 64-65, 71, 74
gathering 30-31, 39, 207
general 81, 168, 259
generally 226
generate 64, 67, 254
generated 64
generation 11, 67
generic 2
geographic 139
getting 2, 52, 157, 233
global 84, 116
govern 125, 254
governance 106, 142, 234, 242
governing 205, 234
government 269
graphical 183
graphics 23
graphs 11

greater 142
greatest 91
ground 72
groups 127, 146, 184-185, 199, 227
growth 71, 112
guarantee 83
guaranteed 34, 263
guidelines 144, 233
guiding 235
handle 174, 198, 215, 239
handled 210
handling 212
happen 27, 120, 209, 215, 223
happened 145
happening 116
happens 10, 32, 51, 114, 126, 188, 199, 242, 265
hardest 47
hardly 252
hardware 192
Havent 207
Having 209
hazards 214
health 112, 114, 255
hearing 119
helping 10
hidden 48
higher 162, 199
highest 20
high-level 40-41
highlight 2, 200
Highly 60
high-tech 105
hijacking 116
hiring 101
historical 188
history 147, 187
hitters 63
hitting 252
holiday 2
honest 121
Honestly 2
hoping 136
horizon 122

humans 10
hypotheses 60
identified 3, 24, 34, 39, 43, 54, 64, 72, 90, 151, 161-162, 164, 168, 177, 185, 190, 199, 201, 214, 217-218, 220, 233-234, 244, 250, 260, 269
identify 1, 12-13, 24, 26, 66, 69, 73, 79, 136, 154, 161-162, 188, 228
ignore 22
ignoring 124
images 150
imbedded 102
immediate 118, 208
imminent 110
impact 7, 34, 42, 46-47, 50, 52-53, 57-58, 86, 126, 142, 148, 190, 207, 210, 212, 220, 230-231, 240, 242, 244, 250, 269-270
impacted 57, 155, 268
impacts 47, 158, 180, 207, 268
implement 20, 56, 73, 92, 148, 199
implicit 119
importance 248
important 22-23, 44, 69, 72-73, 114, 116, 121, 125, 131, 142, 149, 191, 194, 204, 222, 242, 245
improper 235
improve 4, 12, 71, 76-78, 81, 83-88, 90, 136, 157, 175, 187, 192, 217, 236, 260, 268
improved 2, 82-83, 89, 96, 142, 260
improving 82, 226
inactive 186
inadequate 1
incentives 101, 242
Incident 3-16, 18-44, 46-67, 69-103, 106-142, 144-150, 152, 154-161, 164-168, 170-194, 196, 198-212, 214, 216-228, 230, 232-234, 236-238, 240, 242, 244, 246-248, 250, 252-256, 258-263, 265, 267-270
include 26, 85-86, 154, 182, 202
included 4, 10, 162, 180, 188, 212, 224, 228, 256-257, 265
includes 12, 178, 223
including 27, 29, 32, 43, 52, 58, 61, 97, 99, 103, 136, 161, 198, 220, 244
increase 83, 121
increased 111
increasing 111, 232
incurred 52
incurrence 250

in-depth	11, 13
indicate	67, 101, 120
indicated	97
indicators	46, 54, 61, 72-73, 97, 199, 206
indirect	50, 198, 250
indirectly	3
individual	48, 166, 198, 239, 249, 256, 263
industry	1-2, 96, 118, 185
infinite	116
influence	88, 119, 138-139, 232, 263, 268
influences	205
informal	248-249
ingrained	99
inherent	106
in-house	2, 136, 263
initial	42, 130
initially	149
initiated	112, 188, 230, 246
initiating	4, 111, 134, 157
initiative	13, 196-197, 204, 244
Innovate	76
innovation	52, 61, 83, 99, 111, 113
innovative	130, 180, 189, 224
in-process	61
inputs	30, 32, 45, 98, 137, 147
inservice	262
inside	24
insight	67
insights	1-2, 11
inspection	146, 221
inspired	124
Instead	2, 113
instructed	148
insure	109
integrate	85, 103, 110
integrated	111
integrity	20, 112, 230
intended	3, 78
INTENT	18, 29, 45, 60, 76, 92, 105
intention	3
intentions	234
intents	141
interact	108

interest 122, 227
interested 247, 267
interests 19, 263, 267
internal 1, 3, 41, 68, 109-110, 161, 170, 195, 205
interpret 13
interview 1
introduce 48, 206
introduced 155, 241, 246
invalid 164
inventory 161, 186
invest 65
investing 2
investment 18, 55, 69
investor 45
invoices 165
involve 127
involved 20, 36, 62, 74, 79, 120, 126, 139, 142, 155, 177, 184, 193, 201-202, 216, 220, 224, 226, 254, 262, 265
involves 95
isolated 112
issues 19-24, 27-28, 135, 154-155, 157, 172, 174, 177, 194, 217, 236, 239, 244, 270
itself 3, 22
joining 155
jointly 248
justified 99
killer 130
knowledge 1-2, 12, 29, 41, 68, 84, 89, 93, 97, 100-102, 110, 115, 127, 179, 200, 202, 222-223, 243, 266
lacked 96
laptops 238
latest 11, 162
launching 263
leader 39
leaders 35, 43, 66-67, 101, 123, 128, 193, 205
leadership 25, 40-41, 84, 114, 128, 155
learned 1, 9, 99, 103, 129, 258, 261, 267, 269-270
learning 93, 99-100
lesson 261, 267-268
lessons 9, 86, 99, 129, 258, 269-270
Leveling 168
levels 20, 27, 43, 72-73, 96, 102, 114, 162, 214, 250
leverage 30, 84, 99, 128, 181, 188

leveraged 41
levers 222
liability 3
licensed 3
licenses 163
lifecycle 65
life-cycle 50, 263
lifecycles 85
Lifetime 12
likelihood 78, 83, 142, 213
likely 78, 99, 113, 123, 125, 191, 211, 213, 233
limitation 58
limited 12
Linked 31, 232
listed 197
listen 130, 238
little 2
locally 88, 112, 164, 216
located 164, 216
location 233
logical 174
longer 1
long-term 102, 125, 130
looked 1
looking 23, 186
losing 57
losses 33
maintain 92, 112, 135, 190
maintained 85, 161, 262
makers 80
making 81, 84, 86, 88, 123, 196, 208
manage 35, 39, 49, 54, 58, 71, 73, 76, 78, 84, 87, 110, 124, 136, 139, 149, 152, 168, 182, 184, 187, 206, 222, 236, 244-245
manageable 38, 84, 164
managed 10, 40, 61, 68-69, 77-79, 89, 255, 259
Management 3-9, 11-16, 18-44, 46-104, 106-142, 144-150, 152, 154-161, 164-168, 170-194, 196, 198-214, 216-228, 230, 232, 234, 236-238, 240, 242, 244, 246-248, 250-256, 258-263, 265, 267-270
manager 10, 12, 27, 33, 40, 115, 121, 144, 164, 193, 216-217, 219, 227, 259
managers 4, 133-134, 144, 177, 225
manages 88-89, 145, 256
managing 4, 86, 133-134, 138, 234

mandate 136
mandatory 231, 268
manner 162, 229, 246, 248, 251, 259, 263
mantle 122
Manual 234
mapped 40
Mapping 61, 68
margin 165
market 23, 136, 178, 212, 251, 253
marketer 10
marketing 111, 267
markets 27
Master 182
material 137, 161-162, 193-194
materials 3, 269
matrices 152
Matrix 4-7, 139, 152, 198, 212
matter 41, 46, 54
matters 233
maximizing 130
maximum 134
meaning 169
meaningful 106, 162, 199, 249
measurable 31, 39, 136, 224, 234, 249
measure 4, 12, 19, 30, 42, 45, 47-49, 52, 54, 56, 59, 61, 76, 78-79, 88, 90, 92-93, 98, 100, 139, 143, 188, 192, 194
measured 24, 49-50, 53, 55-57, 90, 98, 100, 194, 241, 251
measures 46, 49, 54, 56, 58, 61, 72-73, 95, 97, 101, 214, 224, 242
measuring 92, 199, 234
mechanical 3
mechanics 228
mechanisms 140, 143
mechanized 185
medium 253
meeting 30, 34, 93, 157, 190, 226, 232, 238
meetings 34, 36, 40-41, 148, 211, 233, 270
megatrends 127
member 8, 40, 107, 114, 175, 204, 226, 239, 242
members 1, 31-32, 34, 37-38, 43, 74, 93, 155, 164, 178, 183-184, 202, 205, 216, 220, 225, 236, 238-244, 248-249, 262, 269
membership 240, 249
memorable 249

memory 229
Mentally 148
message 96, 123, 222
messages 204, 239, 245
method 50, 181, 195, 205, 240-241
methods 34, 36, 58, 70, 154, 188, 211, 239
metrics 6, 34, 69, 101, 194-195, 206, 222
Microsoft 224
milestone 5, 170, 173
milestones 30, 70, 138, 146, 173, 263
minimize 142, 183
minimizing 65, 130
minimum 256
minority 19
minutes 34, 238
missed 55, 119
missing 72, 119, 126, 169
mission 62, 70, 121, 201
Mitigate 142
mitigated 2, 260
mitigating 185
mitigation 110, 144, 206
mobile 108, 238, 242
models 23, 67, 121
modified 95
moment 119
moments 66
momentum 119, 121
Monday 1
monetary 21
monitor 93, 97-98, 101, 103, 188
monitored 96, 102, 164, 167
monitoring 8, 92, 94, 99-102, 174, 246
monthly 250
months 1, 88
morning 1
motivate 122
motivation 25, 93
motive 196-197
moving 109
multiple 234
narrative 170
narrow 72

nature 48, 107, 109, 125, 263
nearest 14
nearly 121
necessary 64-65, 67, 70, 81, 108, 121, 130, 141, 158, 188, 211, 225, 230, 235, 243
needed 2, 19-20, 22-23, 25, 30, 66, 93-94, 98, 100, 157, 180, 225, 263
negative 122, 222
negatively 268
negotiate 118
negotiated 128
neither 3
nervous 148
network 6, 172-173, 182, 249
Neutral 13, 18, 29, 45, 60, 76, 92, 105
nonlinear 195
normal 99
Notice 3
noticing 233
notified 206, 265
number 28, 44, 46, 59, 75, 91, 103, 132, 168, 199, 206-207, 271
numbers 108, 122
numerous 266
objection 21, 23
objective 10, 58, 136, 186, 198, 232
objectives 2, 20-21, 23, 29, 31, 33, 62, 70, 95, 103, 106, 114, 120, 124, 127, 135, 142, 144, 191, 203-204, 214, 226, 236, 243, 249
observe 201
observed 87
observing 221
obsolete 127
obstacles 24, 171, 180, 189
obtain 259, 268
obtained 35, 158, 255, 262
obtaining 45
obvious 240
obviously 13
occurred 85, 209
occurrence 206
occurring 90, 210
occurs 19, 94, 246-247
offerings 73, 89

296

office	154, 226, 265
Officer	1
officials	83, 265
offsite	212
one-time	10
ongoing	80, 98, 167
opened	250
operate	190, 229
operates	118
operating	8, 48, 50, 95, 162, 191, 225, 228, 238
operation	102, 234
operations	12, 81, 92, 99, 101, 103, 118, 165, 191
operators	96, 194, 263
opinions	213
opponent	233
opponents	205
opposed	245
opposite	106, 118
opposition	111
optimal	85, 256
optimize	88, 92
optimized	106, 146
option	116
options	27
ordered	1
orders	186
organize	144
organized	168
orient	93
oriented	217
orienting	269
original	161, 183, 216, 232
originally	158, 184
others	134-135, 188-189, 191, 199-200, 210, 260, 268
otherwise	3, 190
outcome	13, 83, 135-136, 140, 175
outcomes	77, 83, 92, 127, 139, 180, 189, 252, 261, 267
outlined	95
output	30, 60, 62-64, 68-69, 99, 101
outputs	32, 62, 65, 69, 98, 139, 174
outside	41, 77, 135-136, 225
outsource	72, 225, 265
outweigh	51, 206

overall 12-13, 21, 59, 103, 114, 124, 173, 194, 223, 233, 256, 261, 263
overcome 180, 189
overhead 161-162, 250-251
overheads 203
overlooked 135, 224, 269
oversight 66, 155, 202, 220
overtime 168
owners 159
ownership 32, 97
packages 161-162
paradigms 124
paragraph 109
parameters 97
Pareto 63
parking 184
particular 67, 263
parties 2, 79, 147, 255, 265-266
partners 20, 36, 79, 98, 114, 128, 140-141, 225
pattern 168
patterns 79
paycheck 122
paying 114
payment 165, 266
payments 262
pending 230
people 10, 24, 52, 57, 70, 79, 90, 99, 108, 113, 115, 119, 123, 126, 128-130, 178, 197, 199, 203, 206, 211, 213-214, 226, 235, 239, 246, 253, 261
perceive 122
perceived 240
percent 126
percentage 123, 152
perception 81, 121, 195
perform 24, 31, 33, 37, 125, 166, 259
performed 50, 80, 152, 162, 166-167, 186, 199, 219, 221, 263
performers 202
performing 209
perhaps 22, 253
period 89, 208, 242
periods 262
permission 3
permit 48

permits 255
person 3, 23, 94, 123, 126
personal	119
personally	152
personnel	21, 25, 96, 126, 165, 172, 182, 196-197, 235, 262, 269
pertinent	96
phases 149, 205, 260
Philosophy	140
phrase 148
pitfalls 106
placed 199, 234
planned	95, 99, 103, 135, 162, 165, 180, 208-209, 261, 268-269
planning	5, 11, 93-94, 141, 147, 155, 157, 174, 212, 226, 246
plates 262
platform	242
players 90
playing 2
pocket 189
pockets	189
points 28, 44, 59-60, 74, 91, 103, 131-132, 170, 196
policies	139, 144, 234, 254, 262
policing	254
policy 33, 83, 87, 158, 174, 263, 270
political	211
portfolio	115
portfolios	204, 244
portion 2
portray 63
position	140
positioned	189
positive	26, 88, 119, 122, 235
positively	268
possess 254
possible	46, 64, 72, 78, 92, 116, 180, 198, 202, 243
posted 254
potential	21, 47, 67, 77, 83, 90, 109, 120, 127, 155, 161, 206, 214, 220, 246
practical	70, 76, 79, 92, 226-227
practice	213, 216
practices	12, 65, 79, 99, 101, 184, 259
praise 240

299

precaution 3
precede 172
predict 228
predicting 92, 139
Prediction 168, 209
predictive 51
predictor 199
pre-filled 11
Premium 206
prepare 200
prepared 1
presence 140
present 102, 117, 131, 185, 212, 222
presented 1, 25, 146, 237
presenting 238
preserve 41
pressing 135
prevent 57, 157, 164, 225
preventive 214
previous 41, 171, 194, 256, 261
previously 145, 230
prices 219
primary 48
principles 144, 243
priorities 49, 52, 58
prioritize 212
priority 52, 168, 199, 223, 248
privacy 37, 145
Private 263
probably 175
problem 18-19, 21-22, 24-27, 29-31, 41-42, 54, 68, 70, 226, 241, 252
problems 19, 21-22, 24, 26, 28, 84, 88, 90, 97, 122, 194, 197, 270
procedure 162, 165, 177, 228
procedures 12, 86, 94-97, 126, 161, 174, 183, 185, 192-193, 197, 220-221, 233, 238, 250
process 4-10, 12, 30, 32, 37, 40-42, 54, 61-64, 66-74, 79, 87, 93-94, 96-97, 99-102, 134, 136, 141, 145-149, 152, 154-157, 174, 177, 181, 186, 192, 196-197, 206-207, 212-213, 220-221, 224-225, 232, 236-237, 246, 251-252, 254, 256, 258, 260, 263, 270
processes 1, 40, 58-62, 66, 68, 71-74, 99, 101, 141-142, 146, 158, 213, 222, 224, 229, 231, 234, 259-260

produce	1, 62, 141, 174, 226, 237, 260
produced	88, 141
producing	152
product	3, 47, 72-73, 125, 130, 154-155, 178, 183, 190-191, 206-207, 211, 215, 224, 226-227, 230, 236, 244, 252-255, 258, 260-261
production	80, 111
productive	198
products	3, 25, 53, 120, 123-125, 136, 143, 149, 152, 162, 194, 225-226, 231, 241
program	19, 50, 68, 103, 108, 136, 141, 143-144, 186, 200, 224, 246, 262
programme	141
programs	204, 226, 228, 244
progress	37, 53, 88, 103, 110, 123, 142-143, 164, 188, 196, 225, 234, 238
prohibited	162
project	4-6, 8-11, 21, 23-24, 33, 49, 65, 68, 74, 85, 95, 98, 106, 113, 115, 120, 122, 127, 130, 133-142, 144-147, 149, 152, 154-160, 164-167, 170-173, 175-193, 198-206, 208-212, 216-217, 219-227, 230, 236-237, 240, 244, 246-248, 252-253, 255-256, 258-261, 263, 265, 267-270
projected	190, 250
projects	4, 58, 126, 133, 135, 140, 142, 152, 160, 165, 177, 186, 199-200, 204, 207, 212, 217, 226-227, 236, 244, 252-253
promising	130
promote	52, 262
proofing	87
proper	98, 161, 199
properly	32, 43, 229, 234, 251
proponents	205
proposal	170-171, 218
proposals	177, 218
proposed	20, 46, 79, 83, 145, 219, 256
protect	69, 114, 145
protection	130
protocols	126, 192, 239, 255
proved	259
provide	19, 67, 107-108, 138, 145, 150-151, 162, 180, 189, 241, 247, 250
provided	2, 14, 102, 218, 254
providers	79
providing	98, 138, 170, 183, 269

provision   232
Public 140, 263
publicity   70
publisher   3
pulled 126, 199
purchase   10, 237, 263
purchased   161
purchasing   1-2
purpose   4, 12, 135-136, 154, 189, 191, 196, 232, 248-249
purposes   145
pursuing   2
pushing   115
qualified   37, 60, 62, 68-69, 74
qualifies   63, 74
qualify 72, 74
qualities   23
quality 6, 8, 12, 47-48, 54, 65-66, 69, 85, 95, 98, 109, 134, 141, 143, 164, 184-185, 190, 192-196, 201, 203, 211, 221, 224-225, 233-236, 263
quantified   96
question   13, 18, 29, 45, 60, 76, 92, 105, 110, 141, 196, 238
questions   10-11, 13, 70, 154, 181, 244, 269
quickly 12, 67
quotes 219
radically   74
raising 141
ranking 229
rather 48, 251, 267
Rating 184, 242
ratings 218
rationale   233, 250
reached   22
reaching   127, 178
reactivate   113
Readiness   165, 222
readings   97
realism 219
realistic   22-23, 74, 131, 144, 183
reality 206
realize 2, 54
realized   124, 259
realizing   1
really   10, 24, 31, 147-148

reason 106, 124
reasonable 84, 119, 144, 186
reasons 33, 194
re-assign 168
rebuild 130
receive 11-12, 40, 48, 120, 236, 245
received 37, 109, 240
receives 242
recently 118
recipient 25, 265
recognised 78
recognize 4, 18-19, 21, 23-24, 27, 79, 83, 86, 240
recognized 19-21, 25-26, 28, 185, 204, 241
recognizes 27
recommend 113, 124, 156
reconciled 263
record 197
recording 3, 238
records 113, 161, 250, 264-265
recovery 58, 70, 106, 209
recurrence 214
redefine 22, 40
re-design 70
reduce 45, 158, 198, 208, 232
reduced 214
reducing 93, 111
references 271
reflect 68, 93, 101, 103, 162, 220
reform 49, 107, 123, 142
reforms 20, 46, 58
refreshed 2
regarding 25, 119, 123, 149, 218, 220, 226
Register 4, 7, 138, 208-209, 244
regret 84
regular 36-37, 256
regularly 34, 38, 41, 190
regulatory 28, 193, 221, 236
reimbursed 238
reinforced 225
rejected 228
relate 66, 231
related 23, 52, 72, 98, 204, 229, 244, 252
relation 23, 26, 78

relations 109
relative 103, 248
relatively 113
release 165, 205
releases 257
relevant 31, 50, 67, 200, 212, 236, 262
reliable 34, 117, 214
reliably 241
relieved 2
remain 36, 269
remaining 188, 268
remember 181
remunerate 87
renewal 254
repair 202
rephrased 12
replace 51, 260
replanning 161
replicated 261
Report 8, 85, 97, 164, 226, 237, 248, 256
reported 129, 149, 195, 252
reporting 62, 98, 114, 161, 248
reports 2, 48, 93, 138, 144
repository 216
represent 90, 230-231
reproduced 3
Reputation 124, 140
request 8, 70, 202, 218, 228-231
requested 3, 86, 228, 230
require 30-31, 49, 60, 95, 174, 183
required 22, 25, 29, 34, 40-41, 48, 65, 80, 82, 84, 96, 167, 169, 172, 181, 203, 208, 210, 247, 254-255, 263, 268
requires 135
requiring 138, 266
rescue 112
research 23, 114, 130, 267
resemble 219
reserved 3
reserves 220
reside 91, 186, 216
residual 161
resistance 222
resistant 264

resolution	67, 78, 154
resolve 19, 22, 27, 168, 236, 238
resolved	194
Resource	6-7, 157, 168, 174-175, 178, 185, 202, 226, 239
resources	2, 4, 10, 19-20, 22, 34, 43, 64, 66, 82, 96-97, 100, 105, 116, 129, 135, 139, 144, 155, 168, 172, 175-176, 181-182, 188, 225, 235-236, 242-243, 249
respect	3
respected	263
respond	142, 222, 238
responded	14
responders	112
response	19, 23, 96-97, 100-102, 222, 257
responses	84, 122, 209
responsive	180, 189
restart 81
restrict 151
result	72, 85, 88, 90, 155, 188, 190, 230, 249, 266, 268
resulted	100
resulting	72, 161
results 11, 31, 38, 73, 76-80, 83, 85-86, 89, 97, 102, 141, 143, 146, 168, 178, 182, 186-188, 192, 198, 243, 258, 260
Retain 105
retained	67
retention	54
retrospect	126
return 88, 116, 172
returning	118
revenue	19, 52
revenues	48
review 12, 62, 149, 183, 233, 242
reviewed	42, 157, 195, 208, 216, 254
reviewer	240-241
reviewers	240
reviews 173, 198, 207, 254
revised 65, 100, 162, 214
revisions	266
revisit   233
reward 48, 52, 69, 226
rewarded	20
rewards	101
rework 51, 55
rights	3

robustness 170
routine 93, 250
safeguard 139, 262
safely 215
safety 23, 118, 124, 239, 254-255
sample 219
satisfied 119, 258, 260
satisfies 252
satisfy 135
savings 33, 54, 65, 262
scalable 80
scenario 33, 38
scenes 2
schedule 5-6, 38, 53, 99, 113, 161, 164-165, 173, 177, 182-183, 190, 198-199, 202, 208-209, 213, 216, 231, 237, 250, 257, 269
scheduled 193, 202
schedules 183, 209
scheduling 162, 184-185, 202, 216, 220, 248
scheme 101
Science 71, 181
scientific 181
Scorecard 4, 14-16, 225
scorecards 101
Scores 16
scoring 12
Screen 228
seamless 109
search 112
second 14
Seconds 238
secret 2
secrets 1
section 14, 28, 44, 59, 74-75, 91, 103, 131-132
sections 193
sector 253
secure 264
securing 57, 129
security 85, 98, 103, 138, 158, 230
segmented 39
segments 38, 127, 250-251
select 74, 103
selected 81, 144-145, 188, 212, 250
selecting 68, 119, 220

306

Selection 7, 218-219
self-help 2
sellers 3
selling 112, 170, 251
senior 101, 114, 128, 193, 248
sensitive 40, 51
separated 251
sequence 166
sequencing 107
series 13
serious 112
seriously 140
Service 1-4, 10, 47, 79, 81, 96, 130, 136, 155, 190-191, 226-227, 234, 263
services 3, 25, 31, 52, 54, 108, 112, 120, 187, 250-251, 256-257, 259, 263, 265
setbacks 67
setting 113, 131
set-up 246
several 70, 212, 262
severance 234
severely 70
Severity 209
shared 101, 188, 232, 251
sharing 89, 100, 134, 250
shifts 26
shopping 1
shorten 182
should 10, 18, 20, 27, 34, 37, 41, 47-48, 65, 67, 69, 71, 74, 79, 82, 87, 90, 98, 100, 103, 106, 113, 129-131, 137-139, 142, 144, 146, 149, 166-168, 175, 177, 182, 190, 193, 200, 206, 208-209, 212-214, 218-219, 225, 231, 236-237, 242-243, 269
signature 129, 262
signatures 174
signed 155
signers 265
silent 238
similar 33, 41, 63, 73, 89, 147, 168, 187, 195, 217, 245
simple 113, 249, 253
simply 11, 232
simulator 241
single 109, 251
single-use 10

situation 2, 27, 45, 186, 253
situations 94
skeptical 111
skills 27, 70, 115, 125, 134, 146, 178, 202-203, 210, 213, 240-241, 248-249
smaller 141
smallest 19, 88
soccer 1
social 111, 140
societal 125
software 25, 149, 162, 182, 192, 207, 210, 257
solicit 36
soliciting 238
solution 1, 56, 67, 70, 76-77, 79-82, 86, 89-92, 155, 215, 256
solutions 49, 77, 83, 85, 89, 94, 213
solving 241
Someone 10
someones 241
something 121, 144, 158, 190, 207
Sometimes 49
source 7, 106, 117, 123, 126, 186, 214, 218-219
sources 32, 63, 213, 262
special 102
specific 11, 22, 31, 33, 39, 69, 112, 122, 157-158, 166, 171-172, 174, 176, 186, 190, 192, 200-201, 227, 231, 235, 263
specified 127, 161, 261
specify 241
spending 2
spoken 118
sponsor 23, 147, 220, 236, 258, 267
sponsored 39
sponsors 20, 222, 248
spread 96, 102
stability 154
stable 255
staffed 43
staffing 27, 101, 157, 184
standard 10, 96, 174, 178, 216, 251, 256-257
standards 12-13, 94, 96, 99, 185, 192, 194-196, 220, 231, 263
started 11, 172
starting 12
startup 137
stated 109, 119, 200, 254, 261

statement   5, 13, 84, 88, 146-148, 154, 156, 221
statements   14, 28, 30-31, 44, 59, 68, 75, 91, 103, 132, 149, 196, 234
static   228
Status   8, 162, 164, 199, 226, 237, 245, 252, 256
statutory   236
steady 57
steering   157, 202, 220
stopper   150
storage   229
stored   242, 264
stories   26, 39
strategic   52, 86, 103, 114, 203, 242
strategies   90, 100, 111, 123, 142, 206, 232
strategy   21, 37, 48, 51, 78, 81, 90, 97, 105, 124, 128, 141-142, 147, 186, 202, 205, 233, 250, 263
Stream 61, 68
strengths   184, 239, 259
stretch 113
strict   66
strive   113, 177
striving 136
Strongly   13, 18, 29, 45, 60, 76, 92, 105
structure   5-6, 49, 85, 106, 113, 117, 154, 156, 159-160, 175, 212, 249
structured   117, 164
structures   141, 248
stubborn   118
stupid   116
subject 11-12, 41, 148
Subjective   194
subjects   60
submit 262
submitted   230
subset   19
sub-teams   243
succeed   52, 114
success   19, 27, 30, 36, 38, 42, 50, 56, 59, 78, 83, 86, 90, 100, 107, 112, 116, 120, 130, 172, 187, 206, 211, 222, 226, 232, 241, 261
successes   125
successful   1, 71, 90-91, 102, 110, 120, 126-127, 134, 141-142, 175, 191, 222, 227, 244

succession 99
suffered 240
sufficient 141, 212, 229, 242
suggested 97, 230-231
suitably 234
Sunday 1
superior 1, 202
supervisor 239
supplier 88, 108, 235
suppliers 32, 61, 73, 128, 220
supplies 259
supply 57, 170
support 3, 10, 81, 93, 98, 102, 108, 111, 135, 150-151, 174, 185, 201, 235, 239, 257
supported 66
supporting 84, 98, 193, 221
supportive 201
supports 239
supposed 198
surface 97
SUSTAIN 4, 88, 105
sustained 186
Sustaining 101, 170
symptom 18, 55
system 12, 31, 68, 70, 99, 111, 117, 128, 136, 149-151, 157, 161-162, 211, 220, 229-230, 234-235, 242, 250-252, 255
systematic 48-49
systems 1, 48, 60-61, 66, 69, 77-78, 101, 154, 165, 224, 252, 258
tackle 55
tactics 232
tailored 2
taking 52, 227, 238
talent 62, 114
talents 115
talking 10
target 32, 116
targets 113, 224, 252, 262
tasked 97
teaming 239
technical 84, 126, 134, 151, 170, 218-219, 254
techniques 67, 121
technology 1, 51, 89, 96, 130, 140, 142, 178, 209-210, 239

templates 10-11
tender 262
testable 39, 150
tested 20
testing 83, 97, 163, 211, 221, 270
thematic 139
themes 249
themselves 1, 48
theory 93
therefore 214
therein 250
things 82, 117, 187, 217, 260
thinking 73, 77, 113
third- 79
thorough 91, 231
thought 205
threat 24, 109
threaten 140
threatened 110
threats 1-2, 157
threshold 193
through 65, 128, 154, 206, 233, 235, 248
throughout 3, 65, 131, 173, 270
Thursday 1
tighter 111
time-based 161
time-bound 31
timeframe 188
timeframes 22
timeline 61, 146, 195, 231
timely 31, 120, 162, 212, 228, 235-236, 246, 251, 269
timetable 173, 263
together 130, 238
tolerable 214
tolerance 149
tolerances 90
tolerated 166
tomorrow 122, 135
toolkit 1-2
toolkits 1-2
topics 85
toward 93, 227
towards 2, 67, 142

tracing 148
tracked 154, 165
tracking 42, 103, 157, 185, 193
traction 111
trademark 3
trademarks 3
tradeoff 219
trade-offs 185
trained 43, 193
training 20, 24, 63, 88, 94, 97, 101-102, 144, 178, 200, 222, 227, 242-243, 262
trainings 25
Transfer 14, 28, 44, 59, 75, 91, 97, 101, 103, 132, 212, 223, 256
transition 116
translated 39
trends 69, 72-73, 122, 195
trigger 78, 90
trophy 122
trouble 108
trying 10, 116, 136, 149, 214, 235
two-page 178
typical 244
ubiquitous 116
ultimate 131
unable 118
unaware 1
unclear 39
uncover 198
uncovered 2
underlying 85
understand 30, 61, 134-135, 148, 200, 207, 241, 254
understood 77, 84, 109, 249
undertake 62, 206, 208
underway 86
unique 2, 170
uniquely 244
Unless 10
unopened 161
unplanned 239
unprepared 1
unpriced 198
unresolved 174, 217

unrest   125
update   1, 190, 267
updated   11-12, 68, 164, 173, 229
updates   12, 101, 120, 256
urgent 30
usability   91, 121
usable 251
useful   86, 98, 159, 269-270
usefully 12, 19
usually 1
utility   180
utilizing 1, 86
validate   55, 252
validated   40-42, 62, 64
Validation   252
Validity 150
valuable   10
values   101, 128, 140
variables   69, 99, 233, 243
variance   8, 240-241, 250-251
-variance   191
variances   161-162, 177, 198, 220, 251
variation   18, 31, 63, 93
variety 90
vendor 134-135, 165
vendors   68, 79
verbiage   247
verified 12, 40-42, 64, 146, 170
verify   47-51, 53-57, 92, 100, 102, 143, 191, 253, 265
verifying   48, 53, 58
version 257, 271
versions   30, 37
vested   122
viable   94, 159
violate 158
violated   157
Violation   158
virtual   242
vision   128, 201
visitors 30
visualize   166, 181
voices   138
volatile 84

313

waited 2
walking 2
warranty 3
weaknesses 140, 147, 170, 218, 259
website 238
weeknights 1
whether 10, 95, 130, 136, 201
-which 210
widespread 94, 101
willing 207, 210
windfall 147
within 1-2, 62, 89, 156, 161, 167, 199, 210, 227, 230, 243, 258
without 1, 3, 14, 112, 130, 230, 266
worked 134, 245, 247
workers 119, 178
workflow 233
workforce 27, 127-128
working 2, 95, 99, 157, 270
work-life 200
workload 207
Worksheet 6, 180, 188
worst-case 33, 38
writing 149, 152
written 3
yesterday 24
youhave 183
yourself 107, 116, 131, 225

Made in the USA
Las Vegas, NV
08 September 2022